Günter von Hummel

What about the ONE

Siri Hustvedt, queer Literature and an Advice for
Selfanalysis

The cover picture, done by T. Heydecker, has the title: 'he.biss.kuss' (as in: he.bite.kiss). The hibiscus blossom, which the word- and letter-play initially leans to, is immediately visible in the middle – in a beautiful, luminous red-violet. But, what about the bite and the kiss? These are seen next to the flower, in the form of a predator's bite, so that the viewer quickly searches for the kiss that would relax the situation again. But for now, there is a lot going on in this picture – men's legs, women's legs are seen, many hands, other flowers, and of course, the kiss – although hidden somewhere in the picture. The whole thing is reminiscent of Kundry's kiss in R. Wagner's Parzival. For Amfortas, as well as in Parzival, this kiss leaves a wound. All of this fits well with the book, which deals with the man-woman relationship, and which plays an important role in Siri Hustvedt's novels. And so, clarity is found in what is written on the back of the cover, the logics of the word-play, the visualization of the subject matter are already anticipated in the attempt at uniting the symbolic and the imaginary in that: 'what about the ONE'.

Production and Publishing
BoD- Books on Demand, Norderstedt, Germany, 2019
ISBN 9783750403581

Table of Contents

1.	Jeanne D'Arc and the Queerness	5
2.	ONE, man and Woman	26
3.	The Dead Father and the universal Woman	51
4.	Siri Hustvedt	71
5.	Queer and Women's Literature	86
6.	Matriarchy and Separation Rage	101
7.	Memories of the Future	116
	Appendix	146
	Bibliography	153

1. Jeanne D'Arc and the Queerness

Jeanne D'Arc, the Virgin of Orleans, was a queer figure, as one might say today. This is due to her penchant for men's clothing and her striving for male heroic deeds, even if one could classify all this as harmlessly neurotic - just as in today's manner. Neither do I want to reduce her greatness. It is well known, that even as a child she heard 'voices' that initially advised her to strengthen her faith in God and in the Church. Later, however, a man with 'snow-white wings' appeared to her, who turned out to be Archangel Michael and called her to fight against England. It was he who promised her where to get men's clothes and how to go to the king. Strict Catholicism and male rule dominated life at that time, and so everything first took its typical, contemporary course, which was rightly not called queer at the time. Such designations were not yet known. But Jeanne D'Arc's appearance was unusual, strange and certainly worrisome for her parents.

Nevertheless we can give a somewhat different assessment of this 'heavenly girl' and her fascinating personality from today and from today's science, especially from psychoanalysis. According to this, there really was something neurotic-hysterical about her and a certain trans-gender tendency can be attributed to the case of Jeanne D'Arc from today's point of view. The preference for men's clothing and also for masculine perseverance still played a decisive role at the very end, when Jeanne D'Arc had been in captivity for a long time. There she had put on her soldier's trousers and jacket again, and it came to a dispute, to a longer back and forth with the prison staff about whether she had clothed herself in such a manner only to protect herself from male intrusiveness, or not. Jeanne D'Arc definitively never thought of wanting to be a man in the sense of a largely male identity. But male attributes attracted her strongly. And why was it the Archangel Michael, who is always represented with male attributes. Such as with sword and lance, and not some other pious figure? Nevertheless, Jeanne D'Arc was also a saint.[1]

Efforts to change sex have only become stronger with the possibilities of physical (hormonal and surgically) alignment. But the man/woman, the transgender theme, has always existed. Already the Greek visionary Theiresias was transformed into a woman by Zeus' wife Hera, and when Hera transformed him back into a man after ten years, Hera asked the well-known silly question, who now enjoys loving more, man or woman, he should now know it as the optimal transgender, Theiresias said: ten times more as a woman! Promptly Hera struck him with blindness, for she certainly did not want to hear that. After her husband produced one affair after the other, she wanted to prove to him that the women didn't have so much of it at all and that the whole thing was just a man's rampage of pleasure. Zeus softened Hera's condemnation to blindness somewhat and lent Theiresias the gift of the visionary.

And so, to this day, history is full of stories of men wearing women's clothes, concealing their homosexuality

---

[1]I write 'saints' in quotation marks because holiness has always been difficult to classify, but one can leave it that way.

or preferring feminine styles. And history is also full of masculine women who act boyish, who 'wear their trousers at home' as they say, or who are even the perfect dominatrix. Indian psychoanalyst, G. Bose, claimed that basically everyone, man and woman, has a transgender desire, and so, in return for Freud's definition of the Oedipus complex, he developed the complex of "opposite wishes" or affects. He contrasted the boy's castration anxiety postulated by Freud, for example, with the unconscious and libidinal "desire to be a woman". The therapist then had to make the patient aware of this unconscious desire and reconcile it with the external situation. However, Bose often got into conflicts when his patients fought too hard against his criteria.

It is not difficult to imagine how a young girl, raised on a farm, would grow into fantasies filled with strength and greatness, spirituality and recognition. Even today, some girls prefer knight games and adventurous activities with boys and thus do not fit into the scheme of pink girl's dreams that many children wish for, or rave about flower arrangements. To be obsessed with being a soldier, to ride on horseback, to have successes, to fight and to win is a bit more unusual. It was astonishing that city commander Baudricourt and also Dauphin, the later king, were persuaded by Jeanne D'Arc to dress her and bestow her with escorts. In today's techno- and bureaucratic world such extraordinary and courageous steps would no longer be possible. Saints nowadays would end up in psychiatry. Indian psychoanalyst S. Kakar described it this way: person who is considered by us to have a personality disorder would be a saint in India and conversely an

Indian saint like Ramakrishna would be regarded by us as "psychotic".[2] However, this opposite is too sweeping and psychologically not thought through enough.

One could also accuse Jeanne D'Arc of a hypomaniac defence. Such an unconscious defending of oneself means that one manoeuvres oneself into an elevated mood and activity, because one wants to defend oneself against a questioning of one's own self-image. Then it is not so much the libidinal desire that is in the foreground, but something aggressive. After all, there is no doubt about the military zeal of Jeanne D'Arc, and one can ask oneself: how does a young girl from the country get to imagine how she penetrates her enemies with her sword? Even if you consider in Freudian manner, that penetrating is part of male sexual behaviour, there is still a hypomaniac-aggressive element to be found in the pictures of Jeanne D'Arc with armour, sword and lance, with which she fended off overly male libido.

But these are all speculations. How would Jeanne D'Arc feel today? 'Hearing voices' at a young age is still common today and it doesn't have to be pathological at all.[3] Jeanne D'Arc certainly didn't suffer from a schizo-affective psychosis, and so only a certain neurotic basic

---

[2]Kakar, S., Der Heilige und die Verrückte, Religiöse Ekstase und psychische Grenzerfahrung, Beck (1993). (The Holy and the Crazy, Religious Ecstasy and Psychic Boundary Experience)

[3]Stratenwerth, I., Stimmen hören, Botschaften aus der inneren Welt, Piper (1999) (Listening to voices, messages from the inner world)

attitude remains, which one could probably attest her today, which has always predestined for artistic or other special achievements and which then can end more or less well. Perhaps the overambitious women who storm the executive floors today are similar personalities. Here in Germany, a second woman has already succeeded in occupying the highest position in the military arena, that of Defence Minister. Fortunately, young women are also rushing forward in philosophy, justice and the financial and economic disciplines, because it is not always a question of mental defence if one wants to be successful.

It is also well known that Jeanne D'Arc, in an outstanding manner, defended herself in court against the intrigues and refinements of the English avengers, but ultimately fell victim to the superiority of the political power struggles between the weak French king and the English. The intrigue was terrible. She was asked trick questions such as whether she was aware of her graciousness. If she had answered to be in the state of grace, she would have been interpreted as heretically arrogant, if she had denied it, she would have admitted her guilt. Pulling herself out of this noose, she said: *"If I am not, may God take me there, if I am, may God keep me there"*![4] A brilliant defence!

The protracted interrogations and trials were constantly about life and death, obsession with faith and misbelief, theological presumption of office and natural, girlish feminine openness as well as numerous other opposites and contradictions. Nevertheless, the question remains:

---

[4]Wikipedia: Jeanne D'Arc

did Jeanne D'Arc not have a minimal queerness, an implied transgender problem, the essence of which has not yet been solved for us here and now. Don't some people with a transgender wish today feel as Jeanne D'Arc did? For example, when a transgender woman struggles to free herself of all masculinity in order to achieve womanhood, only to then not be fully recognized as a woman? One is no longer burned today, but is one not left alone in terrible identity conflicts? To what extent do we all have to deal with this?

Of course, there is a connection between the gender problem and neurosis, Freud already said that the former was the shadow form of the latter. But it does not explain everything. If one has classified Jeanne D'Arc towards the end of her captivity as a 'notorious heretic' and condemned her to death, the whole thing is based only on power-political wars. Perhaps people have been hostile to identity for millennia and have not tolerated forms of self-being that are considerably subject-related. Anyway, for a further clarification, I suggest a small mental experiment.

How would it have been if Jeanne D'Arc had not revoked her confession, which she had already made to a large extent, when she had come to freedom and returned home? Away from English influence, completely under the protection of her chauvinistic French friends, she could then have said that a confession had only been forced through terribly cruel torture, that she now wanted to do everything she could to take further action against the enemies of France. Surely she would not have had the reputation of the great saint, but perhaps she could have preserved that of the political icon. The pyre is only for blatant sadists, whose punishment she could have demanded then with all their might. For oneself the stake is something horrible and atrocious.

Even better that could have been done by the Bohemian reformer Jan Hus, who had been assured of a free conductus (salvus conductus) for his appearance at the Council in Constance. But involved in theological subtleties, he was also burned at the pyre after long tormenting. He, too, could have easily revoked it and returned home to ignite a great popular uprising against the Catholic Church. This did indeed take place in the same way, because the indignation about the nefarious betrayal and the purely politically motivated execution overturned. But finally it was Luther who finally dealt the church the necessary blow.

The times were different and a rigid, murderous superego left these poor disputants of faith no other choice. Or was it the Freudian IT that Jeanne D'Arc imposed the lust for the transsexual and Jan Hus the lust for envy against the stubborn Catholic clerics in Bohemia who were attached to wealth and gluttony. Hus was a strict ascetic, so that he turned numerous poor merchants, shoemakers, hatters, goldsmiths, wine merchants and innkeepers against him. His self-castigation, too, probably stemmed from the onslaught of early desires, which he had to completely repress. He wanted to offer himself to his father as an exaggerated pious man to his rival brothers.

Today, of course, there are immeasurable freedoms that allow one to wipe off everything from one's soul, to talk, to write, or even to be completely absorbed in queerness . I don't understand the term queer in a negative way, it is an expression for the far-reaching 'the other way round' as opposed to what is established in whatever form. Certainly, if you have turned the wheel of habits, rules, compulsive rituals and above all the so-called professionalism at universities and state institutions completely 'the other way round' (and 180 degrees are enough), you are back where you were before. That's why one would have to say it today: queerness is not really queer enough yet, it hasn't really come far enough.

Queerness is making waves, but does not trigger the tsunami that would be necessary to put an end to these rigidifications and horrors that were raging in the world then as they are today, and so my comparison of these two persons from then and now is not very earth-shattering and convincing. I see only the one possibility of all this to come out, which was probably always the best, but was probably hardly used: namely to begin first, as very first, as an individual alone, as an individual with himself and his unconscious and not with others.

That means a beginning exactly with what many newer psychoanalysts today regard as preexisting anyway: the predominance of primary mirroring, especially those in one's own body, i.e. the strong 'mirror-ego', the psychic 'concrete original object' (COO), which determines us from the beginning. [5] It is only then that the actual self-reflections follow, with which one reflects outwardly in

---

[5]Ferrari, A. B., From the Eclipse of the Body to the Dawn of Thought, London: Free Association Books (2004)

the Other. In short: it's about the very place where an individual starts or has to start with himself anyway before the world and society join him. I'll write more about this later, more detailed and understandable.

First I try it again with Lacan, even if it is perhaps less understandable when he says that it is about 'what there is - in each of us and at his most subject-related point - of the ONE' (qu'il y en ait de l'Un).[6] With this, Lacan wants to mathematically formulate this isolation, where everyone begins or must begin, and which, by the way, represents the same isolation as when dying, because it is expressed most precisely. But here are a few examples to explain what this strange statement of Lacan is supposed to mean. As much as Jeanne D'Arc, for example, was isolated in herself, she surrounded herself with holy figures right at the beginning and built up a soldierly following in order to succeed. She didn't expose herself to the body's own mirror, the 'psychic original object' (COO), for long and quickly she went out into the full. So she could neither be one with God nor with the world and certainly not with both in ONE.

Jesus had also taken twelve followers, he did not sit down first of all as an individual, as an isolated person, in Nazareth under a carob tree or under a Tabor oak and waited to have to fulfil the claim of this mysterious 'father' who had sent him to fulfill immediately. At any time someone would have come who would have joined

---

[6]Lacan, J., Séminaire XIX, SEUIL (2011) p. 132 and 239 – 243 as Comte rendu from 9. 2. 1973

him and whom he could have listened to intensively with 'knowing silence' (as the psychoanalyst does when he listens to his patient), in order to gradually bring him to the point of recognizing the great truths. Wouldn't it have been better to start alone as an individual, isolated in himself, and not to immediately make revolting speeches through the regions? Even today he is accused of having been only a social revolutionary.[7]

Now it could have been the case that Jesus had already gone through a phase of isolation, separation and asceticism with John the Baptist, with the Qumran-Essenians or other mystical groups, and only then went out into the world. Hence a different, perhaps better example: wasn't Otto Hahn's nuclear fission so different that he shouldn't have announced it to the public right away, but should have shared the great discovery first of all only with his friend Lise Meitner as a common secret? Only gradually would it have been possible to discuss it in specialist circles and find ways of continuing. It would have been time to discuss all the risks that nuclear fission had made visible and to initiate only reliable people into the matter.

In addition, as far as the relationship with Lise Meitner is concerned: only the secret that two people share makes them a couple, as Sartre once said, and that would have been doubly exemplary: physical discovery and personal intimacy. Well, that sounds silly, but considering how badly Lise Meitner was excluded from the Nobel Prize, how little she was recognized, a little pair building would

---

[7]Augstein, R., Jesus, son of man, Hoffman & Campe (1999)

have been quite good. Starting from both of them as discoverers of nuclear fission, they would then have proceeded cautiously as if they were initiates, and could have postponed the stupid Nobel Prize by years.

It may sound utopian, but would the atomic bomb have been spared for the time being? Another example: S. Freud also founded the 'psychoanalytic society' far too early and gathered followers around himself, when his method was classically suited to proceed from the unconscious of himself as an individual to the unconscious of another individual, among whom then again - not necessarily everyone - but again only one individual could have progressed scientifically with a completely new version of the concept of the unconscious. The psychoanalyst and his client or patient - no matter what one calls it - are in fact an intimate couple from the front, sitting together for hundreds of hours of conversation, and are unable to publish anything about them at this time, because the truth of their being together is only established at the end.

Why didn't the Freudians initially pass on this intimacy in the form of constant, progressive pair building? Later, Freud had to realize that among all the students he had analyzed himself, fights for direction broke out that endangered his method and in some cases even fundamentally damaged it. So he had to write in his book 'Das Unbehagen in der Kultur' (The uneasiness in culture) that it is not by the culture, but in the midst of the culture - and by this he meant quite clearly his already overflowing culture of comrades-in-arms and successors - that causes uneasiness, difficulties and misinterpretations. But it was already too late. The culture had already become a big club where people agreed on what should and shouldn't apply in psychoanalysis. This is still the case today, when psychoanalysis is taught scholastically in many institutes as from above, even when normopaths, the 'dull normals', the well-behaved, are preferred in the selection of training candidates.[8]

So wouldn't Jeanne D'Arc have been better off using a mission only once for herself, building a 'castle of souls' within herself like Saint Theresa of Avila did, or writing books like Hildegard of Bingen? What is the sting in all these people and why don't they clarify their stinginess before they go out into the world? It is often difficult to distinguish between the too early and the too late step. Because if the early step is really as I indicated it with this very early physical ego mirroring, it is obviously - if at all - only done by a few. Lacan may make an exception, having adhered to the concept that I favor here with the demand for initial isolation. He didn't try to make anyone a psychoanalyst by examining them, but to let them become therapists by the way of accompanying persons, so called 'passeurs', who are co-decisive towards a jury. He always said that in the end the psychoanalyst

---

[8]Cremerius, J., Vom Handwerk des Psychoanalytikers, from-mann-holzboog (1990) (From the handicraft oft the psychoanalyst. „The admission filter to education is passing today primarily `normopaths' (Bird, 1986), conservative, adapted contemporaries, `dull normals' (Kernberg, 1984), who essentially have in mind the amenities of the economic and social privileges of the upper middle class".

has to appoint himself as a single person, he has to take this decision as an individual and go his own way.

So Lacan dissolved his psychoanalytic institute, his 'école freudienne', in time for his death. No one should just lie down in a made-up-bed, but should start anew with himself as an individual, with a radical renewal of psychoanalysis, to build a science of the unconscious. All the more, however, his epigones then jumped at the written legacy, and so the same thing happens again: since the writings left behind are very extensive and not easy to read, his sentences were and still are quoted simply without creating a comprehensive renewal from what they contain. Instead of becoming bad epigones, as was the case with Freud, they became good plagiarisers. They, too, do not want to go through the unconscious in these early, still quite physical reflections as isolated individuals.

I would have to stop writing here and pretend that I knew everything better and knew something about 'What about the ONE'. In addition to my psychoanalytic work, I have long occupied myself with meditative methods - from the general psychological and even more from the Indian and Asian cultural circle -, learned them myself and practiced them daily and finally developed a method which I call *Analytic Psychocatharsis*. I have spent thirty years doing this. I oriented myself a little to the philosopher Michel Serres, who died recently, and to whom things were so similar. He was a mediator between intellectual and natural sciences, scourged the parasitic exploitation of nature by man and also took a long time until he became a "career changer and cross-over in contemporary philosophy".

"He did not believe that debates would advance thinking. ... He considered the age of criticism and commentary to be over. From then on, he also saw the meaningful in philosophy on the side of "lonely research and quasi-scientific provision of new adequate concepts".[9] Exactly in this sense of the isolated, the lonely researcher, I also try to stay with myself and to progress, even if not yet with full success. But progress is more important than success. I have written several books, but most readers do not implement the method.[10] That's the only thing that matters to me, but if it is good, it will assert itself by itself. Do I now begin to come as an individual to myself to 'What about the ONE'?

An example of success and progress would be the philosopher J. Habermas, who, in addition to his theoretical studies, was committed to a progressive communicative society and also participated early in the practical success of the student movements. It was not until later that "understanding, that is the guiding principle, is laid out in the language itself. Habermas believes in 'the objective spirit of intersubjective transaction between originally socialized subjects'and in

---

[9]Haniman, J., Gute Laune als Denkprinzip, SZ, 3. 6. 2019, p. 9 (Good mood as a principle of thought)

[10]It has perhaps something to do with the resistance known in psychoanalysis, one is interested in one's own unconscious, wants to read something about it, but does not want to uncover it completely.

'transcendence effective from within'. [11] Has it now become too abstract after all? A book by him with over 1700 pages is to be published before the end of 2019; won't the initiated be the only ones to read it? Should he have remained even more pragmatic, an attitude he opposed to the academic 'Critical Theory' of the Frankfurt School? It's not enough isolation.

Although Habermas had a positive attitude towards psychoanalysis, he called it "therapeutic criticism", which sounds a bit sobering, objectified and cool. He also accused Lacan of 'deliberately obscuring the light of the Enlightenment', which shows that he did not understand psychoanalysis and especially Lacan at all, because enlightenment, rational thinking, is not the therapist's business alone. On the contrary: in psychoanalysis, too much rationality is regarded as a defence mechanism, so one must rightly darken the over-bright, overboard rational thoughts somewhat. Isn't Habermas the scholar in an ivory tower, from whom no one will be able to bring him down today, of course? He will remain one of the greatest universal thinkers. One can acquire outstanding statements from him, but if one wants to approach not only the socialized but the actual subject, one must - as it was also said by Serres - 'through self-reflection', self-sublimation (refinement, elevation, spiritualization), that

---

[11]Schloemann, J., Das Bessere versuchen,(Try for the better), SZ vom 18. 6. 2019, p. 11. (My interpretation: The human subjects are already incorporated and exchange themselves among themselves in such a way that 'objective spirit' arises).

is, completely from within, beginning with 'What about the ONE'. Enlightenment, rational thinking, helps here alone and by far not.

I am only a small psychotherapeutic David compared to Habermas, this spiritual Goliath, but I try to show a way how one can come to 'What about the ONE'. It is clear that starting to count simply with 1,2,3,4,5 etc. cannot be the last wisdom of mathematics, although it is a model for defining unity, wholeness, totality, in short: the ONE, ancient Greek ἕν (hen) for all kinds. Plato held lengthy discussions in Parmenides, but ultimately left the reader to recognize what the ONE is supposed to be. And that wasn't so bad at all, because my point is that everyone has to find it within himself ('transcendence effective from within') and so best of all doesn't have to become followers, disciples, epigones of anyone. Through the usual language - and certainly through an academic, abstract scientific language - it will never be possible to convey something to another. Everyone has to go through 'What about the ONE'.

I came to these thoughts and to the above-mentioned procedure when one morning without visible external cause a tingling, shivering through, 'trickling through' attacked me, as one usually experiences with a moving piece of music, when it grasps you through and through and runs down your back. It's about what is modernly called a chill-out experience[12] A tingling relaxation experience, a relaxation bought at a high price in the

---

[12] Conversation with the doctor and musicologist E. Altenmüller in FORSCHUNG 2 (2012), pp. 14-16

wellness area of a luxury hotel. By the way, the beginning of Brahms' Symphony No. 3 with the wider and wider opening wind chord is supposed to trigger such a 'trickling or shivering through', or such a chill-out experience, which does not differ from those of other primeval times. But in my case no external cause was visible. I hadn't even sat down to meditate, but maybe the intention was enough.

In general and also more soberly, this light sensation of a tingling or 'trickling' shower is understood as an atavistic reaction, which has to do with deep emotionality and was probably an essential communicative reaction for the early humans. These people were still highly sensitive to environmental and speech sounds, which are said to have been similar to murmuring, singing and purring. Apart from a few vowels and just as few consonants, the first humans did not master differentiated articulation. But they heard 'voices', because as I will write from the paleoanthropologist Czarnitzki, they could recognize fir or pine "at the sound of the wind in the needles", naturalistic 'voices'.

They still communicated with the 'inner touch', a kind of 'coinaesthetic inner sense', which has much to do with this early body mirroring, by transferring their connection to nature to the interpersonal interconnectedness.[13] The author quoted here means with a feeling from within, a kind of 'be shining through' from one's own body mirror,

---

[13] Heller-Roazen, D., The Inner Touch, Archaeology of Sensation, Zobe Books (2007).

from the unconscious image-real, a 'feel-real', going one's inner self outward. However, I proceed speculatively here when I describe it as communication from one's own 'It Feels, Senses, Radiates' to one 'It Feels, Senses, Radiates' in the Other, relying only on paleoanthropologists such as Appleton, who proceeds intuitively here. He says that one can only learn something from these early humans if one loves them. Bone remains simply do not provide enough evidence, but perhaps one can combine love with paleo-anthropology in a science subordinated to love.[14]

I must first resort to such comparisons in order to make clear how this 'trickling through' arrived at me. With this experience I had just shared, I was without any thought of any method, had not yet got up completely and was therefore all the more amazed at what was happening in the morning. It reminded me, however, of Goethe's saying in Faust, where it should go down to the realm of the mothers and Faust is overcome by a certain trembling: "The shivering is mankind's best part". And he continues: "Just as the world gives him the feeling, he feels deeply the monstrosity. I would rather understand it as the first part of a self-sublimation,[15] the image-real of one's own body mirror, while the word-real would be the

---

[14]Appleton, T., Warum verschwanden die Neandertaler? Heyne (1999). (Why did the Neanderthals disappear? The author tries to describe and use love as a category of knowledge).

[15]Freud also derived sublimation (refinement, spiritualization) from the Eros-Life instinct, which then does not lead to faster satisfaction, but strives for higher goals (work, art, etc.), but also as self-sublimation for self-improvement.

second part, where it would be about the body echoes to which I later want to comment.

Perhaps the trembling of the well-known writer Siri Hustvedt, which she described in detail in her novel 'The Trembling Woman, a Story of My Nerves',[16] was also such a shudder, a shivering, a kind of atavism or 'feel-real', which has to do not only with the realm of the mothers, but with the deepest unconscious, which arose at a time when man developed an unconscious and thus only really became man. The prehumans, the primacies, the Australopitheci, did not yet know the relationship between the self-body and the self-in-the-Other - mirroring, the symbolic order of which has been established in man and correlates well with this shivering before the monstrous.

Again shortened: The early mirroring in the body takes place without any relation to the outside, a mirroring from something in the body to something different in the body (probably mainly in the brain) is a sensory radiation isolation. Only later, self-reflection in the Other begins,[17] which, if now language is added, enters with reverberation effects, body echoes. Even the infant can usually reproduce the rhythmic sound sequences that have been babbled to him, i.e. confirm or acknowledge

---

[16]Hustvedt, S., 'The Shaking Woman, a History of My Nerves (2011)

[17]The Other, is the meaningful Other internalized from the outside. It no longer stands for the isolation of the pure body mirror, its internalization correlates with the echo-like sound sequences, phrases that echo in the body.

this first it, there or that. Psychoanalyst D. Birksted-Breen points out cases on the basis of which it could be clearly proven that people who lack this ability to 'resonate' cannot dream and therefore usually also have severe sleep disorders and psychological problems.

In order to give an overview of the many terms I use and mostly very similar or the same ones, here is a table, in which I have set down another, shortened pair of terms as the topmost one, which for the sake of simplicity will still often be used.

Narcissus	/	**Echo**
mirrorings		resonating effects
imaginary singifier		symbolic signifier
body-own-mirror		self-in-the-Other-mirror
It Rays		It Speaks
image-real		word-real

Siri Hustvedt is certainly a modern Jeanne D'Arc who shows the men's world what weapons she has. They're not a woman's weapons, as one stupidly always says, meaning her erotic attraction. They are the weapons of the male dominated neurosciences and psychiatry, the weapons of her literary knowledge, her books and lectures. She doesn't have to wear men's clothes, but she has to put on the jargon of the male scientific language. As I will show, this would not be absolutely necessary. In the following I will comment on this several times and also explain what the difference of the above-mentioned pairs of handles is about, how and why the procedure called *Analytic Psychocatharsis* could be developed from this experience, further training, scientific reading and essayistic literature and what all this has to do with the mysterious 'What about the ONE'.

2. ONE, man and woman

Siri Hustvedt is known for her imaginative novels, which are often full of references to neuroscience, psychiatry, philosophy and psychology. In her books she usually also appears herself and many figures from her family of origin play important roles. In the book 'The Sufferings of an American', her alter ego is not only Eric, a psychiatrist, through whose humanity and expertise she can apply all her knowledge and give space to the many disturbed people who she is always interested in. Also in other characters Siri Hustvedt reflects herself and her father, whose original diary she uses as an important and interesting legacy of Eric's father. A lot of neurotic, strange and mysterious things happen in this book and makes it exciting.

In her most recent book 'When feelings meet words', she proceeds differently, but on the same multi-layered level. Here, too, she doesn't spare her tremendous reading and her claim to science, and often picking up on highly diverse details. [18] She is interviewed by Elisabeth Bronfen, who is very close to her soul and asks exactly the good questions that Siri Hustvedt can use to express the universe of her far-reaching diversity of thoughts. Bronfen has philosophized about what the writer E. Allen Poe announced in 1846: "The death of a beautiful woman is without doubt the most poetic subject on earth". Strange! Bronfen extends this statement almost to the

---

[18]Hustvedt, S., Wenn Gefühle auf Worte treffen (When feelings meet words), Kampa (2019)

necrophiliac 'beautiful female corpse'.[19] Siri Hustvedt's poly-scientist and autobiographical statements are not quite as profound as all of her novels, which deal decisively with the relationship between man and woman, where she adopts a predominantly feminist attitude and discusses the relationships of her characters from a neuropsychological point of view.

In another interview, for example, she said: "It is very important for a woman to discover masculinity in herself as well as in others. This also applies to men in mirroring and self-images. We must integrate all aspects into ourselves in order to be complete beings.[20] That sounds simple, but at the same time a bit overarching. Because if you combine all feminine and masculine aspects in yourself, are you then - as she once says elsewhere - androgynous (or in a modern term: postgender)? Doesn't that sound too little differentiated, too en bloc, too generalizing? Of course, Siri Hustvedt has given even more detailed information on the subject of man/woman; I will come back to the many literary and technical descriptions and theories.

On the other hand, Lacan's statements regarding the same problem, namely the relationship between man and

---

[19]Bronfen, E., Nur über meine Leiche: Tod, Weiblichkeit und Ästhetik (Only over my dead body: Death, femininity and aesthetics), Königshausen & Neumann (2004)
[20]Mayer, S., Siri Hustvedt, „Warum lieben sich Menschen? Ich habe keine Ahnung" ("Why do people love each other? I have no idea."), ZEIT online vom 17. 3. 2011

woman as quite complicated, too difficult and too complex come across to the interested reader. This already begins with the fact that he points out a hundred times in his work that the gender relationship man/woman does not exist at all. It is not really logical, clearly differentiated, definite, clearly symbolically determinable and therefore existentially not comprehensible. It happens, it floats around and one can also talk about it, but one says nothing with it, verifies nothing and establishes no founded saga, no essential work of human culture or science. Gender relations thus remain an unfinished piece of theatricality.

Now Lacan 'is not to be understood', is the résumé of many readers of his seminars, and often psychoanalysts are also present who say this. The language that plays such a central role in Lacan, they argue, is not the unconscious one. That is only one aspect. But Lacan also claimed something completely different. He said that the unconscious was structured, that it was built up l i k e a language, like the language of the image-word-real which I mentioned above, where part of the word (the It *Speaks*) represents Lacan's 'L'Autre (The Other). This capitalized Other is the internalization of all the important others (parents, educators, teachers, superiors, psychoanalysts, etc.).), not only in the form of a compulsory or superego, but also in the form of multi-layered inner-soul 'objects'. This all leads to an echo, an echo discourse that is different, but also speaking, which causes difficulties for a unity of the soul, but also makes it possible.[21] This also applies above all to the first body mirrorings, the very first ego emergence, the image and gaze-real and their combination with the word-real.

It is precisely this insinuated unity that is particularly difficult to make out in the field of man/woman, male/female. Siri Hustvedt nevertheless works on it in her books with obsessional ambition, it is almost her exclusive subject, genre and goal, and undoubtedly in this way she also proves something like the impossibility of gender relations. In her novels, rough, uneducated and sexist men are usually confronted with artistic and sometimes even slightly spunky women, which destroys or almost brutally destroys any 'in-betweenness'[22] - as she calls it. For she too knows that the relationship between the sexes is not so easily determined literarily, nor scientifically, and thus tries it with hermeneutic terms she has created herself.

Lacan, on the other hand, likes to allude to psychoanalysis as 'logical practice', to mathematics and

---

[21]Lacan gives the Other many names: Witness of truth, place of unconscious desire, place of lack of being, the analyst as deadly silencer, main place of the symbolic, field where the subject receives his message in reverse form, possibility of 'jouissance', etc. But it is precisely in the form of primary, rhythmic, echo-like sounds, of an It pronouces, It *Speaks* that a combination with the equally primary reflection of the body, the It *Rays*, is possible. Combination means: closest connection like 'What's about the ONE'.

[22]Whether this is the original denomination in S. Hustvedt's English, I could not find it determined anywhere.

topology as the pinnacle of wisdom, and often expresses himself in such a way that it often gives the entirety the character of the rather complicated and abysmal. To man and woman, for example, however, he also says very simple things again. The woman, for example, he says with regard to the relationship with the man, is not only his 'alter ego', but also more the play maker of the relationship and more the power symbol than himself. She i s Φ (Greek Phi), 'phallic Symbol', erotic metaphor, heraldry of lust, primacy of sexual relationship, while he only has Φ, un-relatively strong and perhaps better written in small letters, which is probably an allusion to the so-called small difference that really exists, even if both sexes participate equally in the phallic (Freud's phallic phase of childhood).

"The woman is the symptom of the man," continues Lacan, "because she is the moment of truth for him".[23] For the psychoanalyst, the symptom of mental illness is a hidden, but nevertheless, very relevant truth. This truth is often so far and so deeply repressed that it can no longer be discovered. As far as the truth itself in a general sense is concerned, it is - as so often - mainly about the relationship between man and woman, and men are the better repressors. So it is easier for the man - as Lacan further notes - to be confronted with a male enemy on the level of rivalry than with the woman on the level of competition, which fits well with the fact that he misappropriates more understanding and knowledge in his relationship to her. The man thinks that a male debate,

---

[23]Lacan, J., Seminaire XVIII, Seuil (2006) pp. 34-35

a male dominated discussion, a militant man-to-man exchange, is more interesting - albeit more painful - than a dialogue with a woman who sensitively perceives things, discusses them in many layers, but with regards to which he believes that one cannot argue with her and therefore does not progress.

To the extent that the woman is the support of this truth, it is also true, according to Lacan, "that in the relationship between man and woman there is only appearance. . . . but when it comes to understanding something, namely that if you want the truth of a man you would do well to know who his wife is, here I mean: his wife, and why not? This is the only place where there is any sense to what someone from my environment once called the 'personal scale'. To weigh a person there is nothing better than to 'weigh' his wife - when it comes to the man". Menetekel - 'weighed and found too light'? Weighed and found who he is?

Well, there is still much that remains unclear. Perhaps it would be better to refer to Lacan's Seminar XIX (Comte rendu of February 9, 1973), where he made this strange remark about "What about the ONE" (also shortened and written in French Yad'lun), even if it was even less understandable. Lacan insists that in order to begin counting one cannot begin with One (ancient Greek μόνος, monos), even more with One (ἕν, hen, this more comprehensive concept). In the end, however - as today's set theory has also shown - one must begin with multiplicity, i.e. at least with Three, in order to arrive at 'What about the ONE' in retrograde steps. L'Un, ONE, is substantiated, and thus it can be avoided that one simply says: "There is ONE". For the "there is" would give the ONE an ontology, an immediate existence, a firm presence.

But precisely this is to be avoided. ONE must be founded by each individual for himself, in himself and through himself (that is, subject-related). Is it perhaps because Siri Hustvedt does not find a final solution for the woman/man relationship, for the gender relationship, because she sticks with the two? In man and woman, in normal and neurotic, in educated and uneducated, all the dichotomies she uses. Siri Hustvedt is extremely well-read, informed, educated, but sometimes she also uses it as a weapon. No, she quotes plenty of scientists, neurologists, psychiatrists, philosophers in contexts that are not yet known, and here she is really a researcher, a discoverer, a platform of revelation, where pure mathematics does not play such a major role. But perhaps it would help her after all?

Nevertheless, why the Three? On the occasion of a visit to London Zoo, where a lion was surrounded by three lionesses, Lacan was again concerned with mathematics, but it was a mathematics of Eros, i.e. what Siri Hustvedt's letter also revolves around. But according to Lacan's comment, this surrounded, idolized, amor-ensnarled lion could not count to three, on which outraged listeners protested. The lion would know exactly that he had three lovers. But in a purely arithmetical sense, Lacan was right. The lion does not count, he does not sum, he has no 'relation' to the three, to the threeness. For him three are simply several, many, several of the same kind and apparently sufficient. Nothing else is needed. "There is

ONE," so you can't say as I said, because that's what you're stuck with. It has to do with what Lacan calls the ONE-Science, the Henology, where it's about the more comprehensive approach, and what he read about Plato's Parmenides. "L'UN", ONE, 'ex-sists' at first, i.e. it 'sists' (insists) from 'ex' (from the outside). ONE is not existing ontological (if I may say so even more stupidly than Lacan does).

It may sound a bit like the transcendent, but Lacan wants to avoid philosophy, he wants It, the Freudian It, the subject, let It be said to himself. Ex-sistence, then, is something other than existence. In Lacan's case, this statement comes above all from the fact that there is, as emphasized, no gender relationship, i.e. nothing that can be said, verified, defined or - as he also says in this compte rendu – "quantified" by the relation, the relationship of the sexes man and woman. One can't grasp the ONE or the common or superordinate or the XY of the sexes, even and especially not when they want to become one.

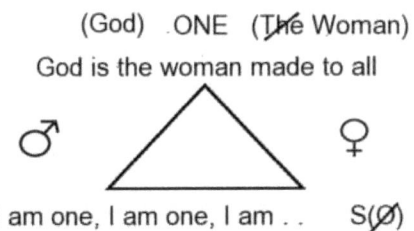

(God) ONE (The Woman)
God is the woman made to all
I am one, I am one, I am . . S(Ø)

To put it simply, the sexes are staggering around each other and don't find ONE where life is actually happens, and so it remains the appearance mentioned earlier, in which man and woman go each their own way.

This is really nothing completely new. Only the emphasis on the fact that sexual relationship does not have at all correct existence, because it always goes wrong, because the man always comes too early and doesn't know what to do a the crucial moment , has probably not yet been expressed so definitively. All this does not mean that there is no sex, there are encounters, events, all that is constantly in modern novels, but there is no logically expressive, concretely irrevocable thing. All this can be seen in the above rather odd triangle illustration. At the top is ONE, which I have described with (God) on the left and with (The Woman) on the right. Below is Lacan's sentence: "God is the woman made to all". The matter becomes clearer when one looks at the two lower corners of the triangle.

Below left is the man who brought speaking into life by "emphasizing repeating" sounds, but in the sense of speaking predominately of himself.[24] I am One, I am Lord, I am One, I am. . . just as Robinson Crusoe did when he found the Indian on his desert island and said to him: "I Lord, you Friday". After all, he had to pronounce some-thing, and then he had to say something that clarified the situation. This imperative language is probably a male invention. The philosopher G. F. Hegel, with his dialectic about lord and servant, has also written a contribution on this subject, which has resulted in the

---

[24]It says that the first words were not names for things, but calls for identity and stressed repetitions.

fact that the lord first of all has renounced certain pleasures, even if he has thus surrendered himself to death through lustlessness. The servant, on the other hand, does not want to renounce anything, but he must of course wait for the Lord's final death in order to get at his possessions.

It is clear that the man with this stubborn repetition of the one and the emphasis of his masterhood, with the infinite counting of the number, never reaches the greatness and height of "What about the ONE". He only counts himself to death. But on the woman's side it is not much better either. In Lacan's formulation she strives to be the signifier of the barred Other, O, the great, high, real Other (L'Autre), but which - as said above and further expressed in psychoanalytical language - only exists castrated (therefore written cross-stroked), blocked, inhibited. For otherwise it would be what one has called God, the All-One who towers above everything, in short what one has always more or less mythically told: the theological myth of "What about the ONE", monotheism as a simple statement.

After all, the woman, who was already the "image of God" for Thomas Aquinas (while the man was his mouthpiece), is close to the top right corner of the square. But she is not the woman who represents all women (which is why her The is crossed out), she is but one woman, the one only. This is what the problems of the Oedipus complex and also of the original Alpha man in the early days of mankind are all about (insofar as all this has to do with the relationship man/woman in psychoanalysis, where the measure of enjoyment is first and foremost male).

According to Freud, the original alpha-man namely is the one who enjoys owning all women (i.e. believes to own them, but that is not so important here), and the sons, the young men, kill him one day because of it, whereby they raised him up later through feelings of guilt and repentance to a God.[25] It is not the women, but the father/son conflict that gives rise to the unit of measurement with which - unconsciously - counting takes place. It is the same mental mechanism as in the myth of Oedipus, which kills the father in order to finally conquer the woman who seems to represent all of them, namely Iocaste (she is mother, lover, billionaire, femme fatal, fairy, and even queen, in short everything that is conceivable in this respect).

But she doesn't exist so immediately, i.e. she too is 'sisting ex', outside, which Oedipus has to see in the end and finally, blindingly, banishes himself to the shadow realm (on Kolonos). Conclusion of all this: if God were the one who's supposed to be the ONE, he would be - psychoanalytically speaking (and that is what this here is about) - this virtual figure of the woman representing all women. He would be the by a male measurement "woman made to all", i. e. the one who could express them all within himself. But since that doesn't work, it's better to stick with "What about the ONE," a new mathematics in which no one can ever again act by

---

[25]Freud, S., Totem und Tabu, GW Band IX, Fischer (1960)

repeating the simple One, nor dream the dream of the complete Other who would be God.

For the time being, everything what deals with enjoyment remains with the male unit of measurement, since the female is more difficult to determine. To say that God is actually a goddess does not make things any better, because she would then be really the one who represents all women, and that is borderline, not to define, not to "quantify" as Lacan thinks and as it is necessary in science. The religion philosopher R. Spaemann has therefore provided a better definition. He said that God was an "immortal rumour". That was not meant to be negative, because Spaemann is a strict Catholic. But his definition hits the nail on the head. There will always be talk of God, even if he cannot be grasped in reality. A goddess, on the other hand, is not a rumour; one could say, analogously to Thomas Aquinas, that she is a living vision that may die, but can become so intrusive as a vision that one can no longer get rid of her. So you need mathematics that can solve the problem.

And how does one learn the new mathematics that would do justice to men and women? Not quite that fast, because the male units of measurement are speech units, phonemes, signifiers, word real co-determined by Eros, just these emphasized repetitions, echo effects, with which the stronger ones were able to show off earlier - not only with shouting, but also with constant sound sequences. He could make the very first identity sounds of himself, the very first slogans, watchwords.[26] The women did not get their chance until later, and that is still up to them today. I am referring here to linguistic and psychoanalytical guidelines, which I do not have and do not want to discuss further at the moment, because as shown in the triangle above, there is no one-sided and final evaluation associated with them.

So everything is quite simple, transparent, understandable. Why do people make so many problems in regard to their relationships? I am reading another book by Siri Hustvedt, this top American intellectual: 'The blazing world'. In it, she describes the story of a female, artist and her relationships to men, to the art world, and to the question of gender identities, spiced with all the intrigues, loves, and fantasies of New York society. Conclusion: the art world is also male-dominated like many others. This is why it is so problematic to be fully understood as a woman with the art of writing, and this is why Siri Hustvedt tried to justify her 'trembling' with neuroscientific explanations, but also to accept it from a psychological or psychoanalytical point of view. She also went into analytical psychotherapy, where she certainly learned that it is not the man but the father who dominates (although this means least the biological father, but the father as such, the symbolic father, and in psychoanalysis this is usually father Freud).

---

[26] Even in the chirping of birds there are constant sound sequences, but they are not detachable from the reference to action, a difference that I will take up again later.

Well, it would probably have been better to go into Lacan's analysis, considering that the trembling occurred in a public speech after the death of the father, where in Lacan the father symbol stands for the name as such, the actual 'proper name', which is not a name for an identity, but something close to tautology. The father's name or word thus entangles itself in the father of the name, of the word, which for example is best revealed in such a tautological saying as 'war is war'. 'War is war' does not emphasize the facts of the matter, but rather the emphasis on the cruel and warlike. So it has a special metaphorical effect, because the unconscious early mirrorings as well as the resounding effects give war its real cruel name, its proper horrid name. Such a name element also plays a decisive role in *Analytic Psychocatharsis*.[27]

But perhaps Siri Hustvedt was quite rightly afraid that a negative countertransference in a Lacanian psychoanalytic session would have scared her too much. [28] Conventional psychoanalytic therapy can also be problematic for highly sensitive people. With this I am alluding again to the body mirror theorists and the procedure of *Analytic Psychocatharsis*, where is shown how to deal better with it. For it is not for nothing that I have referred in the subtitle of this book to self-analysis,

---

[27]Here the proper name is evoked by meditation of so-called *formula-word*s from the iterative force of the unconscious itself and directly, more detailed later.

[28]The patient usually transfers meanings of inadequate content to the analyst (positive transfer). Anger against him and insult is a negative transmission and the same applies to the counter-transmission of the analyst.

for which one never needs anyone but oneself and something picture-word-real like that I have yet to show.

Even the physical proximity of the therapist sitting directly behind one while lying on the couch can be unbearable. But also it doesn't help to get advice about a lot of neuroscientific and psychological nature and to expect change on the university way. For Siri Hustvedt it was probably hardly a purely hysterical reaction, about which she herself speculates, but there was probably a somatization disorder influenced by it. Because Siri Hustvedt also rightly rejected an organic disease. I tell all this because nowadays it is not uncommon that one knows everything and can get thousands of information through libraries and the Internet without getting to the root of one's own soul in the unconscious of the individual from which I proceeded. Although the language I use at the moment is a wonderful means to talk about everything, but some things cannot be achieved through the word and the linguistically formed thoughts, but only by adding the image and the looks related to it, i.e. the image-real. More details later.

Of course, something unconsciously sexually-aggressive between father and daughter - totally unconsciously phantasmatically shaped - can explain such a somatization, but especially if this abusive did not actually take place, but was awakened by relationship structures (severity or ambiguities, allusions, unclear gestures and above all by unconscious phantasies), it can be the background of the disease and not be recognized. Instead of repressions, direct splits in the psychological play a major role.[29] In any case, Siri Hustvedt is very successful, even her daughter says that her mother always does everything right (so it's not like with the usual families, where the mother is sometimes called the worst mother in the world). The only thing that stands out: Siri Hustfeldt is somehow a little bit bloodless, not properly grounded, too top-heavy, too brilliant, too much - as she herself says - influenced by intellectual defence.

As already hinted at, Siri Hustvedt in the book 'The blazing World' lets the psychologist Rachel say in a conversation with the main protagonist Harriet Burden (called Harry, pseudonym for a real artist) that "intolerance towards certain forms of sexual life can be found everywhere. . . Is it not taboo in our culture to express even a hint of compassion for the man with paedophile desires, or to acknowledge the simple truth that there are sexual encounters between adults and children that leave no wounds in the latter"? So the book is full of subtle, intelligent, lascivious, exaggerating and provocative dialogues, but the fact that paedophilia leaves no harm to children, even if the wounds are so small, is certainly not true. Here the queerness shows it's mysterious face.

---

[29]Lacan says that man is generally divided within himself. "Those who are not divided are crazy," he claims. This psychoanalytical subtlety can best be explained by the fact that the incursion of language into biological, image-real life has created a split with the word-real. The animal has its instincts, which are image-real, but the human being is split and thus normal as a word-real human being.

These statements are probably not only a literary coup or trick, but also perhaps the denial of an abuse that took place in the author's own childhood. She suspects that something has happened to her, but says that she obviously survived it without any wounds, because how else could she be so successful and satisfied. It is quite possible, as I already indicated, that it is one's own early primordial phantasms, the COO, that cause the same damage as an external reality. And what's more: the psychoanalytic theories are boundless, but in practice they are often lacking, so that I don't want to make any definitive statements about Siri Hustvedt's psychodynamics and would understand that she and all the others can't derive anything from my statements.

But the trembling has to originate from somewhere, and Siri Hustvedt herself writes about it openly and in a variety of ways. I think, as I said, one can only explain the whole thing with a far-reaching separation of intensive psychic contents. Judith Le Soldat, a psychoanalyst who turned Freud's theory around and plumbed the depths of extreme erotic aggression, is a specialist for this kind of thing. She describes macabrely and curiously that the Oedipus complex and castration anxiety are not the central elements of Freudian therapy. Rather, the focus is on the sphinx standing between the murderous jealousy towards the father and the Eros infatuation with the mother in the Oedipus saga, the absolute transgender figure, which also has a chimeric character. She is one of the female and mother figures equipped with the animality of eating and being eaten and male sexuality, who plunges the child's soul into unsolvable conflicts at the beginning of life.[30] The child develops libidinous-aggressive aspirations towards her by means of unconscious own imagination, which block each other. Doesn't one feel here the source of the very early mirrorings?

According to Le Soldat, Freud's Oedipus story only provided him with an excuse, a psychological defence, in order not to have to face these violent sexual and sadistic impulses. But as exciting as her arguments are to be read, because she tears Freud's initial dream (the dream of 'Irma's injection') to pieces in every detail, her psychoanalysis can probably only be regarded as therapy in special cases, and so I will not claim in any way that such a treatment would be generally helpful. But as a theoretical contribution Judith Le Soldat's considerations are valuable, because she tackles the decisive interface between the purely pictorial unconscious and the worthy pre-conscious with great libidinal and aggressive monster-like phantasms, which massively set the inner-mental conflicts in motion. One can perhaps not heal them completely, but unravel them better, and so I think that one speaks here better of an unconsciously primary, phantasmatic and unfulfillable addiction to fusion, which often underlies psychosomatic disturbances, and which one can redirect at least by Judith Le Soldat's procedure.

Psychosomatic means that we are dealing with aspects that are particularly deeply knotted in the unconscious,

---

[30]Le Soldat, J., Eine Theorie menschlichen Unglücks, Trieb, Schuld, Phantasie (A theory of human misfortune, instinct, guilt, fantasy), Fischer Sozialwissenschaft (1994)

where one likes to think of extraordinary therapeutic constructs. In the play 'The Net World' by the American dramaturg Jennifer Haley, these conflicting forces are also at stake, and because they are net forces that affect neuro-psychology, they fit in here, i.e. in the context of neuro-science and psychoanalysis. The play is about a pedophile who has created a virtual reality network in which one can pursue all imaginable pederastic tendencies. The girls abused there are computer emulations of real role models, and a lawyer is now to determine whether this is legal or should be forbidden. But the stage, which changes in the theatre between an interrogation room and an abuse room, shows the close interweaving of the two networks, the normo- and the phantasmatic-real, and when the investigator falls in love with the man she sends to the paedophile network world for testing, confusion arises throughout. A legal analysis now seems irrelevant, as well as it is often difficult to draw the line between what is pornography and not.

There will certainly soon be such network worlds, perfect 'active refuges', for which not even pictures of real people have to be used, because everything is AI-generated. But the problem is then no longer just the individual pedophile, who spends many hours a day in his 'refuge' and can still follow a legal interrogation, but that each individual wants to virtually-realize his own boundless fantasies, although they can no longer work together in the standardized real. Perhaps a few porn films do not change the character of the individual, but they do change a virtual reality society in which no one understands the other's addiction.

And so, Siri Hustvedt writes little about such deeply unconscious conflicts in her novels, but somehow about her life, as she often emphasizes herself. She also speaks of the feasts of strong, joyful desire, which encompass a variety of sexual preferences, even practices such as sadomasochism. [31] But aren't we talking here about especially male fantasies, such as those brought into play by the Marquis de Sade and Sacher Masoch? Siri Hustvedt also makes numerous statements about orgasm according to the male model, yes, they even become a female domain because of their multiplicity. In turn the men fall for this concession of the women by the dozen and also deceive themselves about themselves, as also the women continue to leave it puzzling, what their orgasm is really about. In fact, there is no gender relationship and therefore the most adventurous colportages exist about it.

Siri Hustvedt has to write these great, multi-layered and neuroscientifically, psychoanalytically and artscientifically filled novels, otherwise she would be attacked by the sphinx that unites the two sexes without the slightest idea of "What about the ONE". Lacan has made a special effort to speak so complicatedly of henology, of the ONE-science, because otherwise people snatch "What about the ONE", even quickly, as Plato did in Parmenides. There, Plato argued that "the one" (to hen) "cannot be much (ta polla)". . . but "the many cannot be without one either". [32] In short: "There is no ONE (no

---

[31]Hustvedt, S., Wenn Gefühle auf Worte treffen (If feelings meet words), Kampa (2019) S. 109

[32]Platon, Parmenides, Insel Verlag (1991)

existence) except against the background of the not ONE (the non-existence) and vice versa".[33]

At this point I have to come back to the primary body-own mirroring and explain it in more detail. It is the first of the two forms of reflections or mirrorings, in that it is a direct mirroring with one's own body, the pure It *Rays*, narcissus in pure form, the COO or the 'trickling through' ascan be experienced in *Analytic Psychocatharsis*. Psychoanalyst S. Maiello also describes this early form of It *Rays* as an "object of experience", in which the child 'experiences' the warmth and excitement of the mother as its own image-real. And the early form of It *Speaks* she calls the "sound object",[34] because the child 'hears' the mother's heartbeat and speech and also considers this to be it's own rhythmic, echoing, narrative. Now these psychic 'objects' initially connect with each other in a chaotic way. This is probably the reason for the second phase, the one of mirroring oneself in the Other outside and for a more elaborated.

Here, in this second phase, it is about what everyone already learns in school: self-reflection in the outside, of which it is always said that this is the only way to become whole and authentic. Only in the Other can one truly see and understand oneself (image-real) and also name that as an identity (word-real). Alone you are nothing. This reflection contains vanity, narcissism and

---

[33]Lacan, J., Seminaire XIX, SEUIL (2011) p. 134

[34]Maiello, S., Das Klang-Objekt (The sound object), PSYCHE Nr. 2 (1999) S. 137-157

projective identifications, while the word-real expresses itself in the speech composed by the ego and other personal psychic entities. It can also take on superego forms, be a witness of truth or an inner interlocutor as already described in footnote 18. It is specifically this second phase that plays the leading role in classic analytic psychotherapy.

But the first mirroring, the pure body reflection of the primal phase, which takes place in the centre of the human being (mostly in the brain) and which is still too little considered in research, is much more important. The evolutionary biologist C. Wills has developed a model that explains this primary body mirroring as the beginning of being human.[35] He spoke of the "brain that has gone through" or "was rushing ahead" with itself in the context of human development. The enlargement, the complex development of his brain, the multi-layered group dynamics (to which also belongs the longer dependence on the mother), but above all the ascending identity problems would have forced the early or still pre-humans to reorientations, sometimes to the "turning a corner", to behavior reversals and to the loss of innate instincts, he postulated. With all these demands, the brain has hurried too far ahead, it has come to self-mirrorings in its own brain, to spontaneous 'visions', to a space filled with lucidity and enlightenment, but also to a state of excitement, which - cooled down - has made possible the aforementioned, calmer, more constant body-own mirroring (a lust-ego as Freud said).

---

[35]Wills, C., Das vorauseilende Gehirn, Fischer (1996) S. 20

In this context the philosopher P. Sloterdijk spoke of foaming, of foaming over the brain, which comes to the same conclusion.[36] Pictorial impressions have made the human brain 'foam', yes, this psychic proliferation has actually made it human. He now

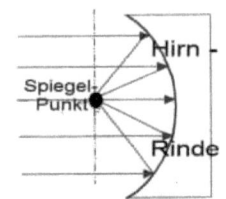

possessed a picture, an - as psychoanalysts say - 'imaginary object', a very first, still unconscious ego. S. Freud had already recognized this when he said: "The ego is above all a physical one, it is not only a surface being, but itself the projection of a surface".[37] Really, a lust-ego.

So it is something like a mirror-gaze, lingering in its own dimension for a certain moment and almost already caught, that appears out of nowhere. This reflection, this primal image of the ego itself, is thus only a projection, something imaginary-real, which psychoanalysts call an 'imaginary object'. It is object and yet also something gaze-like and opaque. In this early mirroring, which already takes place in the mother's womb and immediately after birth for some time further in relation to one's own body, there are also already parts of it contained, whether the child corresponds to more paternal or more maternal genes and whether it is male or female.

---

[36]Sloterdijk, P., Sphären III, Schäume, Suhrkamp (2004)

[37]Freud, S., GW XIII, S. 237 - 289

In a scientific way, the brain is seen as a hemisphere sitting on the base of the skull, i.e. as a concave, internally reflecting nerve cell layer that selectively reflects *Rays* coming from the body and other brain layers in the centre of the hemisphere (see figure). It is the subject and reflection point of images and glances that radiate towards and away from this point without

affecting the physiological visual process. It is the point of curiosity, the It *Rays*. What is important is that it is a purely bodylike, direct mirroring of the individual that occurs in isolation in each individual and - so to speak in a vacuum - forms the core of the first ego in pure surface projection.

I like to try explaining this with the essence of the 'lucid dream', in which one finds oneself in the total mirror world of this body mirror, in virtual space, and at the same time bathes in the 'jouissance', the autochthonous enjoyment. Freud's libido is "desexualized" in autochthonous 'jouissance' like it is this dream state, but visually, virtually, the whole thing can be experienced in the lucid dream in such a way that one considers it real (real in one's enjoyment), and in a certain way it is. Lacan speaks of the 'imaginary-real', the purely topological figure, of which I depict one here (the starry sky as Möbius band).

It is a single contiguous surface, which nevertheless always has two sides. And this is exactly how you get involved every time you travel on one side in such a

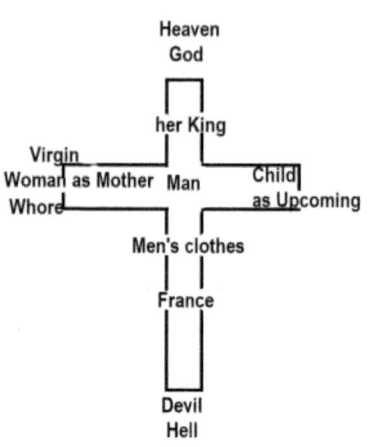

wonderful, marvellous, lucid dream, and then have to wake up or fall back into sleep when you arrive on the other side without noticing it. For pure body mirroring, however, one has to imagine the occurrences in the sense of Einstein's geometry.

Not only Jeanne D'Arc was trapped in such a topology, we all are. My teaching analyst O. Count of Wittgenstein, in a detailed discussion of the essence of Jeanne D'Arc, presented her image-real in the form of a cross with cor-responding symbolizations, the word-real, in its precarious combination. It is about the cross of her youth and that which she held in her hand when dying at the stake. In the sense of nested topology, all words must be understood only as unconscious body reflections in which the vertical and horizontal opposites are conveyed in such a way that they represent the real. Moreover, the woman as such does not exist in this imaginary-real, Jeanne D'Arc apparently already knew that uncon-sciously, she was trapped in it.

3. The Dead Father and the universal Woman

"What about the ONE" nobody can tell you, no author, no scientist and also no psychoanalyst. This can only be conveyed to everyone by the image-real (imaginary-real) of the body mirror and by the word-real (symbolic-real) of the Other in each person himself who, for example, directly provides information in the process of *Analytic Psychocatharsis*. But perhaps it also helps if one has at least a little memory of The woman. Because even if she doesn't exist, she is somehow very alive and the Other isn't completely dead. She is so universal, so multi-faceted, and he is so well known, so deep in memory. I will show, that behind these two figures there are two kinds of psychoanalytic theory formation, the one of the 'dead father' (God) and the one of the 'rich, universal woman' (all representing).

I make the following suggestion: regarding the 'dead father' (the God created from the guilt feeling), Lacan speaks as mentioned of the 'names of the father', of "Les noms du père", which in French also sound like "Le non du père (The No of the Father) and "Le non Dupes errent" (The non-dumb err), the homophony of French has phonetic interfaces. [38] Thus Lacan had created a

---

[38]Siri Hustvedt also quotes this sentence from Lacan, but she knows nothing about the nature of this homophony (unison), although she claims to have studied Lacan thoroughly and have used his theories in her dissertation. Quote from 'When feelings meet words', p. 86). Later she distanced herself from Lacan's ideas (!).

formula-word-like triple formulation which, like the formula-words used in the process of *Analytic Psychocatharsis*, are also tri- or multi-meaningful. This is how the unconscious works, this is how the combination of image and word works, of *Rays / Speaks*. You have to go through something like this in order to come to a real and true statement of the unconscious.

The adjacent illustration shows a formula word used in *Analytic Psychocatharsis* and now written in a simplified circle, in which different meanings can be read out from different letters, just as the three different meanings could be heard in Lacan's sentence. Here the letters are not interrupted according to homophony interfaces  (different meanings produced by phonetic similarity) in Lacan's theorem, but separated by homography interfaces (different meanings produced by writing similarity). One could therefore better call them B(r)uchstaben,[39] since they show the different meanings in a repeatedly cut lettering, as I will show in detail later (page 83). In any case, the principle presented here is clear: three or more meanings by phonetic or pictorial separation phenomena show exactly the three-in-one or one-in-three behavior already described above.

---

[39]Oudée Dünkelsbühler, U., Zeugnis & Schrift: B(r)uchstaben an der Couch, Les Etats Généraux de la Psychanalyse (2001). This is a play on words between letters and broken characters that is possible in German.

Lacan wants to demonstrate that 'What about the ONE' lies hidden behind the Three. But what was only an example of theoretical nature in his lectures is a practical possibility in the formula-word shown above for selfanalysis. If one meditates on it, the unconscious itself must result in 'What about the ONE'. Because there is nobody and nothing in the formula-word precisely, because of the ambiguity or multiplicity of its meaning, there is no clear statement in it, one cannot commit oneself to any For?? even from its non-existence it can stimulate all areas of life, literature, art and science. practice of *Analytic Psychocatharsis*, because in this way the final statement is wrung out of the unconscious itself. In the appendix the whole procedure is also described in brief, so that anyone can start practicing it - and exactly as an individual.

This uniqueness by a single writing written in a circle with simultaneous ambiguity, if one reads starting at different letters, reminds again of the 'rich, universal woman', who seems to represent all women. For even from its non-existence it can stimulate all areas of life, literature, art and science. One does not have to live physically to do that. And so it has an effect just like a formu.la word that represents all sorts of possibilities that - as I said - stimulates the unconscious to reveal its truth. Both, the universal woman and meditation, are extremely vital events, as much as they are purely thematically different.

In analytic psychocathartic meditation, the cathartic experience arises, the flickering of the body-own-mirroring, the radiance and not only the speaking of the truth in question. I came across these things through the well-known myth researcher R. von Ranke-Graves, who staged the cult of the 'White Goddess' precisely around this figure of the 'rich, universal woman'. Because the many myths around Aphrodite, Athena, Hera, Alkestis and a hundred other women from ancient Greece inspired him powerfully to this vision of femininity. In his real life however this 'White Goddess' had something to do with the famous actress Ava Gardner, with whom he was a friend and who was known for her excessive and sibyllic life.[40] So she was - albeit in two halves - actually alive. He also attended witch gatherings of witches and thus probably sought more catharsis or ecstasy than wisdom.

But such ecstatic phenomena are not the predominant goal of my book nor of *Analytic Psychocatharsis*. In whose first practice it comes to the described, liberating experience, detachment and cathartic revelation in the sense of 'trickling through experiences' of the body image and whose correspondence with the chill-out experiences I have already mentioned. But this applies only to the moment of the first exercise in the procedure of *Analytic Psychocatharsis*. In the second, following exercise, the pass-words that appear there correct all these phenomena and expose the truth of the unconscious in symbolic form. So one could say that this cathartic appearance again coincides a lot with the direct mirroring of the body itself, the pass-words on the other hand with the reflection in the Other. Thus the ONE can be represented

---

[40] Ranke-Graves, von, R., Die weiße Göttin (The white God-dess), Rowohlt (1992)

as a combination of both, which however - as already often emphasized - each individual has to create in himself. This is the only way she, the one who does not exist, becomes particularly alive and the Other – even if he is dead - becomes able to speak.

In practice this looks like this: if one repeats several of these formula words purely mentally, the catharsis that is now taking place, the 'shivering through' of the body image, the image-real, serves to lead over to the practice of the 'inner hearing', the symbolic-real of the pass words, i.e. to the second exercise. It is well known that people used to be treated with hypnosis in the past, but they also immersed themselves in this deeply relaxing, oscillating image-real of their own body image, were able to 'see' vivid images of early memories and floated as pleasurably in the aforementioned lucid dream. But this state was totally dependent on the therapist's voice, one could only hear his thoughts, so that people only turned their symptoms into an addiction frenzy. The images remembered in hypnosis were then - awakened again - not of great validity, they seemed to be only half hallucinations, which one did not have to know about.

Freud left this method because he wanted to have the truth for the person who was mature from the outset, i.e. ready to speak and to profess. So it was all the more difficult to get to the early memories without this unconsciously pictorial, unconsciously imaginary. He and the psychoanalysts who followed him had to struggle through endless associations in order to filter out something half confessing. The 'trickling shower of the first exercise of *Analytic Psychocatharsis* on the contrary leads one directly into the second exercise, which opens the unconscious in addition to the relaxing monotony of the formula words. Free associations were no longer necessary. Now the point of the connection of the *Rays / Speaks* is reached as the point of the ONE and expresses itself just pass-literally, from which a confession to the inner truth with a little bit also rational thought help is easily possible.

A literary example. Siri Hustveldt never had to be the 'L'Adultera', the adulteress that T. Fontane so often addresses in his novels. Latin 'adultero' actually means 'I do it differently', and moreover: the male form, 'adult', also means lover. Siri Hustvedt would surely have taken the best literary approach to the fact that the female form means adulteress, while men are ascribed the amorous-positive role of the lover, discriminatory against women. So the injustice is already in the original words. Already in 'L'Adultera', the first of these novels related to women, Fontane lets his main protagonist stand by her adulterous feelings of love, whereby it was clear from the outset that a real marriage had not existed at all.[41] Kommerzienrat van der Straaten loves art more than his wife and has a copy of Tintoretto's 'Adulteress' made for him right from the start: a 'ludificatio', a mockery, a tremendously sarcastic gesture towards the woman. An example so for the word of truth behind the free associations of the story or for a *pass-word* directly extracted from it.

But in contrast to Fontane's later novel 'Effi Briest', the matter turns out well, just as the marriage-breaker in the

---

[41]Fonatne, T., L'Adultera, Greifenverlag zu Rudelstadt (1988)

New Testament - and Tintoretto's painting refers to this - gets away with the life and heartfelt advice of Jesus. Melanie van Straaten loses her position in upper-class society, but finds a home in her love for her new husband and, above all, in very simple bourgeois work, which she confirmed and which the society of the time could not demonise. With Effi Briest the romance ends terribly. After the revelation of her love affair she is rejected by everyone and dies at the age of thirty in her parents' house. Probably because of this unfortunate end, the author D. Keuler, tried to rewrite Fontane's 'Effi Briest'. For Keuler, the fact that Fontane in his "Effi Briest" creates a type of woman who - as he says - "like all my wives have a knack" means that the author brings in his own women's problems here: she does not make Effi Briest unhappy as an adulteress, but "the woman leaves her husband and finds true happiness in the arms of a friend".[42]

The author thus favours a modern, lesbian, a queer solution, why not? That also works like a *pass-word*, like a word of truth. Even if that would hardly have fit in with Fontane's time and gender view, even though Keuler is certainly right that Fontane had a clear problem with women. Fortunately, the real model of Effi Briest, Elisabeth Baroness von Ardenne, after she had died at the age of almost 100, in contrast to the character in the novel, did not become so old out of sheer unhappiness.

---

[42]Keuler, D., Ein offener Brief, in Buchforum Nr.X, S. 49 (An open letter, in book forum Nr. X)

Of course, Fontane was a patristic-paternal type and Freud's sexual-scientific language is also just as patristic-universitarien abstracted, but what is the real truth about women's fates now? What is female identity, what is the love between man and woman? One can clearly see how the imaginary and the symbolic mix significantly, albeit differently, but what is the real of these women? Where is the mathematics of their specific Eros?

Siri Hustvedt probably does not know a final solution, even if she has found an identity for herself in her life, but she cannot directly communicate it in a helpful manner nor transfer it to others. She is not a doctor, not a therapist and has no healing method of her own. As is well known, psychoanalysis focuses not only on transference but also on the transference-related interpretation of 'free associations'. By positively transferring meanings from his own history or from other relationships to the analyst, the patient assumes knowledge from him. This transference of assumed knowledge, however, enables the therapist to interpret the 'free associations' related to him and to interpret their real content. Literature cannot achieve this by itself.

And further: Actually the analyst should not react back, not contrast, but take up the meanings related to him and interpret them in the overall context, interpret them, and thus bring them to consciousness. The transfer / opposite transfer matrix is thus a problem for psychoanalysis if, as already mentioned, the transferred meanings shifted to the analyst are not sufficiently interpreted and thus solved. The right solution here is also a revelation, the coming alive of the 'universal woman' (the living vision) or hearing the words of the 'dead father' (the immortal rumour, if I may bring these psychoanalytical cult figures into play again). Speaking in psychoanalysis does not serve communication, but this insight revealed by liveliness and words. Not only the phonemes, the word reality, are involved, but also the pixels of the image-real.

Transmission (symbolic, word-real) / subordination (imaginary, image-real) sound like the same alternating pair of forces, just as the double of transference/counter-transference shows this reciprocity. Such a connection can best be seen in the well-known phenomenon of 'Déjà vu', which has seen or experienced something like this before. But it hasn't really been seen that way, the phenomenon of 'Déjà vu' goes hand in hand with that of a 'Jamais raconté', something that has never really been told or pronounced before. The 'raconté' of the symbolizing transmission is closely connected with the 'vu' of the mirroring counter-reaction and can thus also be grasped in the psychoanalytical concept of the 'original scene'. The 'original scene' consists in the awareness of an intimate, aggressive encounter from which one was totally excluded, even pushed away - e.g. when looking into one's parents' bedroom as a toddler. It is thus something like the prototype of a trauma. A bad 'Vu/Raconté'.

One of my patients once dreamed of hearing noises in her parents' bedroom, she went there in her dream and saw - nothing! Nobody was lying in the beds. Returning she found her mother - harmlessly busy - in the kitchen. To relive the 'original scene' is so embarrassing that the patient had split her perception and had irritated away the parents who were violently intimate. Exactly the same was dreamed by another patient. He also heard noise in his parents' bedroom, went there and saw: two strangers in their parents' bed! Oh, they must have accommodated guests there, he thought in his dream, before he woke up. What he really saw had become a 'déjà vu', but now a constant dream 'raconté' of all possible paraphrases and detours. The view into the "original scene" is repressed. Many people will still dream that nobody or other people are lying in their parents' bed. The thing is just too embarrassing and too traumatic to remember.

For example, the dreams about the parents' empty or occupied bed also have to do with the therapist and the transmission related to him, because he listens intensely, is fully involved in the events, and so he can see himself as the one who is overlooked here in the bedroom, which is at the moment the speech room. Just as the patient has to fully remember the original scene, he also has to tell his analyst all the resistances belonging to it. The therapist's interpretation will cautiously approach the empty or occupied bed and - if it is not fully accurate - lead to the patient having to continue telling more and more. Therefore one can say that in psycho-analysis the 'symbolic order' of the word-reality is in the foreground, because it has to be talked, talked and talked. Sometimes you have to construct the interpretation, but here, too, more narrative elements play the main role. Elements of gaze and image which are so important after all are contained only indirectly.

And so the phase of the primary body-own reflection is quite different. Here in the mirror of one's own body, the brain, one 'sees', 'sees' and 'sees' again. Lacan calls it the phase of the 'dismembered body' (corps morcelée) with which life begins. The toddler experiences completely uncontrolled movements, disjointed layers of sensation and body reflections. There is still no uniform self-image of one's own ego, since the stability, duration and firmness of the nucleus of a first ego formation is constantly lost or even not properly created by the mirroring phenomena just mentioned. Freud had still assumed that the fragmentation, fractionising, uncoordinatedness in the psycho-physical realm results from the erotic-aggressive combination of Eros life instincts and the destruction death instincts. But this view turned out to be too pessimistic, but also too abstract to be understood as word-real. Here more pictorial-real is indicated, as I emphasize it more strongly in *Analytic Psychocatharsis* and in the depictions shown.

The reformulation by Lacan into the combination of show and speech impulses, which I have already quoted, is in many respects more plausible, if not more pleasing. Similarly, psychoanalyst R. Krause writes that humans are born with two 'organisational cores' of a psycho-physical nature, which cannot always be well held together, 'interconnected', by the influence of the mother, other primary persons or environmental events. These two 'organization cores' are pictorial, visual, pictorial-real (body mirrorings) and on the other hand phonetic, word-real (self-reflection of the Other).[43] Very simplified I speak also concerning these two instincts or 'organisational cores' of the image-real as in the It radiates and a word-real as in the It *Speaks*.

In Jeanne D'Arc, too, the vertical (body-own reflection), the masculine, and the horizontal (girl, mother, child as self reflection in the Other), the feminine, have crossed in an unfortunate way. With today's transgender debates, the question of true psychic reflections has become important and more and more this first, the body's own reflection is coming to the foreground, in which one is very well alone with oneself, even if not lonely and isolated. And this is exactly what one stumbles across in the transgender discussion today. There we always distinguish between sex and gender, where sex is the genetic ascription and gender the psycho-social. But it's not that simple. As discussed, there is with every human being first of all this body mirroring which takes place only in himself, this 'mirror-ego' which already contains almost everything which will later constitute the human being, the same as for sexual orientation.[44]

---

[43]Krause, R., Affektpsychologische Überlegungen zu Seinsformen des Menschen (Affect-psychological reflections on human forms of being), PSYCHE Nr. 6 (2017) S. 453 – 478

[44]I refer to numerous psychoanalytic, body mirror theoretical authors such as A. Ferrari, D. Birkstedt-Breen, T. Ogden. R. Lombardi, R. Carvalho, A. Lemma and others, and the book 'The body speaks' by the latter author gives a good overview of what I will tell more about.

Transgender people completely ignore this archetype, this first phase-like body mirroring, which therefore already contains male or female reflections corresponding exactly to the genetic, body image sex. They refer to an unknown cause, namely that they have the opposite gender identity in spite of contrary biology (and now also in spite of contrary body reflection). They do not accept that environment, parents, other reference persons or influences have controlled the tendency to others, to trans-identity, so that one could change this again by psychotherapy. They are firmly convinced that they possess a different being, a different appearance, a different sexual attitude than the one given. They accept heavy psychological, hormonal and surgical strains in order to carry out a sex change, a total transformation. That's queerness, why not, but isn't it already over 180 degrees 'the other way round'?

This masking of early body mirroring can also be found elsewhere, e.g. in a variety of body-modifying practices. First and foremost, cosmetic surgery applications should be mentioned that are certainly not pathological to a certain extent, but nowadays often go far beyond small, insignificant and not so relevant changes. The most important ones are surgeries, breast augmentations, liposuction, growth changes and the like. But also hair dyeing, piercing, scarifying, tattooing and everyday things like make-up, clothes, eye-catching glasses, tanning through solariums, etc. play a big role in the complex, which is called a dysmorphophobia, a fear of malformation, bad appearance and deformity.

All this is - again emphasized - certainly not to be classified as pathological, but has to do with the lack of a basic body mirror that is not available. It serves to replace the forgotten, mentally split off or denied body mirroring and to integrate it into the second self-reflection, where cultural, social and conscious-psychological motives can be advanced. In most cases, this second self-reflection then turns out to be too narcissistic, even exhibitionistic, as is the case with tattoos or the exaggeratedly fashionable or for other reasons sight-seeing clothing. All harmlessly queer and funny.

Of course, tattoos are intended to appear stronger, more courageous, more dangerous, more erotic, but also more beautiful and more peaceful and loveable with flowery inscriptions. One does not know that the actual signs, symbols, heraldries, signifiers of the body-mirrored ego are much more effective than the artificially created ones. English psychoanalyst A Lemma writes in her article 'The Black Mirror' that this early mirror is covered with body modifications and tattoos because it appeared to people as dark, as black, and so they have to paint something on it or reshape it, because otherwise life is difficult to bear.[45]

In all this hullabaloo, the 'autochthone enjoyment' doesn't really come into its own, which I also see as the most elementary thing with Lacan, that is, exactly what 'there is of the ONE', in the background. Something of the

[45] Lemma, A., Der schwarze Spiegel The black Mirror), in PSYCHE 9/10, 2019

above-mentioned 'jouissance' is always there already, but it's not tangible and certainly not constantly perceivable. Krause, too, showed that the 'connection' of the two 'organisation cores' (*Rays / Speaks*) often fails, because in the relationship to the very early mother (this primordial other), emotional scripts, similar to unfortunate scripts, lead to mental splitting. The original repression or this splitting is not only about a factual process that hurts and has a "sensory overload" effect, but also about something that says no to it, even if this promise is not fully conscious. In Krause's sense, the two psycho-physical 'organisation cores' are not well interconnected, they often break apart again completely, in that a negativity is at work here, a 'no', against which the child does not yet have any arguments, not even knowing how to speak and defend itself.

But no more of all these theoretical and abstract formulations. "Grey is all theory," Goethe wrote, "and green the golden tree of life". A little queer this sentence, but not only because queer is modern, also because it reflects quite well the basis of psychoanalysis (splitting, infantile sexual), I want to say something again about these heavenly girls, as Jeanne D'Arc was one. For example to Hildegard von Bingen. On the basis of her visions, Saint Hildegard claimed that on Judgment Day the otherwise still fixed stars would swirl wildly through each other in order to find a new order. They meet in Lacan's subject or 'radiant' point, in this lucid 'light', which was the main star for Saint Hildegard, the King's Bride, with whom she probably identified herself.

This star is, of course, not a real star at night. For this meditative, visionary observance "does not happen under a starry sky," as the literary theorist M. Blanchot writes, but under the "dés astre", a play on words that has to do with the stars but also with "disaster". [46] For Saint Hildegard, too, the role of the King's Bride was anything but simple. Her overly close proximity to her fellow sister Richardis, who did not want her to move to another monastery and was only willing to do so under duress, shows that there was a second main star. And this relationship is a good example of true queerness. For Hildegard's almost erotomanic love for Richardis of Stade was intense, one can certainly speak of an extreme erotic self-sublimation, a catharsis of *Rays*, of the image-real, and also of the gift of the word-real, of a passport word (namely: to be the bride of Christ), which, however, in view of her passionate love for Richardis, almost led to the "dés astre".

This was the case at times when the saint tried to hold Richardis back in her monastery with all force and all means. When Richardis brother - already knowing about the problem - wanted to convey to her the position of an abbess in another monastery, Hildegard turned to the superiors of the order, but in return the archbishop of Mainz finally forbade her to keep her fellow sister. Richardis left, but the saint did not give up. She called various other officials and even wrote to the Pope, for she knew how to justify her worldly love as included in God's

---

[46] Blanchot, M., Die Schrift des Desasters (The Scripture of Disaster), W. Fink-Verlag (2015) S.67

love, and that is queer. Suddenly lesbian affection should be the will of God, whom Hildegard had otherwise glorified in such wonderful visions, poems and books. The pope gave her a rejection, in the often usual conversion of great love to hatred the saint even tried to accuse Richardis of simony. Hildegard von Bingen still lamented her fate at an advanced age.

All this does not mean that one cannot love God spiritually nor a woman in lesbian manner. But Saint Hildegard von Bingen was extremely absorbed in her spiritual concerns, she enjoyed international fame and at the same time lived in an equally intense erotic passion. Today one would say that one could bring such a conflict situation to professional helpers, therapists, but also to a certain extent to the public. Hildegard could have written down her despair in a book. Finally Richardis had not remained without corresponding feelings, when she was dying (much earlier than Hildegard), she absolutely wanted to be brought back to her monastery.

How conflict situations are solved in the *Analytic Psychocatharsis*, I quote once on the basis of an example of these passport words, of which I have already spoken, and quote later still an open, honest confession of Freud, which - just concerning the truth - shows its true greatness. One of my probands, who had been practicing *Analytic Psychocatharsis* for some time, heard the thought from a distance or as if from depth: "She already has her work clothes," and he knew immediately what it was all about. By 'she' was meant the girlfriend he had known for some time and intended to marry. And the term work clothes' didn't pose a problem either, he told me, because it just consisted of nothing, only her naked skin, the entire surface of the sex appeal. As much as the appearance of such a password surprised him, he was also shocked by the ironic, almost scornful truth of this saying, which degraded his girlfriend to a sex worker.

But he also felt an enlightening surprise regarding the uncouthness and directness of the expression. No friend, no therapist could have told him so convincingly and unmaskingly. Especially no moraliser. Of course, the truth was also mocking, frivolous, a joke among men, but somehow it was also shameful. But above all it belonged to him first of all, and he really liked that. That you can find the truth detector in yourself, he experienced like a small sensation. He felt strongly motivated to tell me about it and to continue with the exercises. But he also told his girlfriend soon after, whereupon they both took a lot of time to talk about their relationship.

Had he always seen her like this? Was it possible to talk openly about the fantasies everyone had about their relationship? How often does one just not come up with the right word, the right beginning of a conversation? You have to call on the Truth Detector within you, but this is not possible in the usual way of a resolution or a too blatant revelation that one doesn't dare. If you can tell a dream, if the other knows how to interpret it, this may be a similarly good start into deep and honest communication. But who can? Even the therapist must often have heard whole dream stories in order to be able to give an accurate interpretation.

On the other hand, the password words, which are triggered by the unravelling structure of the formula words, are an ideal impulse for self-awareness, self-analysis and extended communication. The fact that she "has always had her working clothes," my respondent thus uncovered the lie that women like to work in these clothes. Everything is already there, the girlfriend only has to get started, ironically speaking. My proband knew very well that this was not true, but he hadn't understood it, just as one knows more about the history of the Third Reich or the world wars than about other epochs, but still hasn't understood it. In the unconscious we know everything, even in sleep we often know that we dream, and even if we have understood this knowledge, we have not grasped, realized it. In the passport words we do not always understand it the same and exactly, but they help us to realize and grasp it.

I must admit, however, that good psychoanalysis can also produce excellent solutions, even though I prefer *Analytic Psychocatharsis*. So I want to tell you about Freud's own dream regarding his son in World War I. [47] Freud dreamed of the news of the death of his son, which did not really happen. According to some associations and revealing interpretations, Freud confesses here that despite the "painful emotion should such a misfortune [the son could have been wounded or fallen] really happen", a resurgence of envy against youth, almost a hidden desire to die, could alleviate the pain. This is an

---

[47]Freud, S., GW II/III, S. 564.

incredibly honest and open description of what is simply necessary in any therapy. As much as the conventional psychoanalytic procedure is cumbersome and lengthy, I would advise anyone who is interested in deeply engaging in *Analytic Psychocatharsis*[48] to spend at least fifty hours in analytical psychotherapy and to read the relevant literature in detail.

---

[48]For example: to teach it to others.

4. Siri Hustvedt

The novels of Siri Hustvedt are exciting to read. They are, as I mentioned before, full of spirit, neuroscience, art theory, feminism, gender discussion, and countless other areas, all of which bear witness to great literacy. One of her last books 'A Woman Looking at Men Looking at Women' again deals with the subject of man and woman. The author has taken a critical stance on the painters M. Beckmann and W. de Kooning as well as on the writer O. Knausgard and revealed their one-sided and hopelessly men-oriented outlook on life. One does not have to be a feminist to condemn the rude machismo of the aforementioned men. Admittedly, an examination of the painters P. Klee, F. Marc and G. Richter would probably have revealed more friendly results, but this is not a sufficiently good argument.

One can understand that Siri Hustvedt doesn't think much of Freud's penis envy. More than a hundred years ago this biologistic language could perhaps not be completely avoided, so Lacan speaks in a modern way of Φ (Greek Phi for 'phallus symbolique', sexual pride and power) which is of course only another, somewhat more exalted symbol for the same thing that Freud experienced: the sexual as such, i.e. talking about it especially in its infantile form. Φ is based on the masculine, but applies to both sexes in the same way. But to say it this way remains misleading. In other books I have therefore put Ψ (Greek Psi for unconscious Psyche) on the side of Φ, which is more based on the female side and with which one can easily lead endless gender discussions to a solution. Nevertheless, one still has to make a brief remark about Lacan's view in this regard.

Although Lacan describes himself as a clear Freudian, he emphasizes female enjoyment in contrast to the "plaisier phallique", the male lust contrasting the "jouissance". However, this distinction still leaves the Φ its traditional place since Freud, but no longer so comprehensive, no longer so holistic. Lacan is concerned here with his theory of signifiers, that is, with what I like to call a word-real, a symbolic-real that can always be found in the unconscious in the treatment of mentally ill people. As I quoted above, Lacan's slogan was that gender relation does not exist anyway, i.e. precisely in this word-real it cannot be definitively determined, it cannot be located, it cannot be verified logically, and certainly not 'quantified' (which is Lacan's passion).

According to Lacan, the sexuality that happens in the outward illusory reality is only a Freudian parapraxis, a miss, a slip-up. The man always ejaculates at the height of his anxiety, at the point of no-more-further-knowledge surprising him. And this has to do just with Φ, which lacks Ψ. In the Freudian interpretations, Ψ remains correlating to that as a small remnant, which is about the image-real, about the own-body-mirror. In so far Siri Hustvedt is right naturally, if she describes the weaknesses, the Machismo and the social and psychological disorientation of man's world referred to Φ in detail as good Feminist. There is nothing to gloss over. On another sheet the question stands, why the women do not use their advantages often and estimate in particular their ability for the jouissance, the guarantor of Ψ, which is connected thus with the body own mirroring, so small.

They do not believe in it or "they lack something of the symbolic material", as Lacan sloppily remarked. Well, I don't think you can say it that way. They rather lack what we all lack, namely how to bring Φ and Ψ together in a successful, fitting, ideal form. Because men lack Ψ, the pictorially psychic, the more stable imaginary order or the more controlled image-real, body mirroring, as I would call it, and this is exactly what Siri Hustvedt shows in all colours and shades. But what does she do with Ψ?

For her, Ψ could apply perfectly, in that it creates her 'in-between-ness', the 'space of possibility' (here she quotes Winnikott), in my opinion the peaceful, warm and tender commitment among humans determined by females. But just as the socially idealized forms are not perfectly sufficient and of course psychoanalysis (with Φ) does not solve all social and neuropsychological problems, the Ψ-obligation does not do justice to everything. The double-headed motif in Siri Hustvedt's novels ('the Blazing World' and 'Memories of the Future', where she is always herself and the main character, sometimes with the same initiatives) would be well suited to inventing and literarily expanding a character under the motto Φ/Ψ. But then it would probably be just a fake character again, after all.

As already mentioned Thomas von Aquinas said, the woman is the image, the pictorially radiant appearance of God, while the man has more the role of the divine mouthpiece. But although the woman has this access to Ψ, to the unconsciously psychic image-reality, she usually does not succeed in bringing Ψ enough to common people or to express it in her own way. But what is her way? Doesn't Siri Hustvedt command her way perfectly, people also read her books enthusiastically, but she does not succeed in a therapeutic effect, a healing through the truth, as psychoanalysis claims to do (and which partly does not succeed), neither with herself nor with others.

For a woman who has the more original access to Ψ cannot bring the picture-word reality to people in the same feminine original version, just as is rightly criticized when men like Freud and Lacan want to pass Φ on in the same masculine original version. Lacan tries to deal with this brilliantly with mathematics, topology, linguistics and many other areas, but like Siri Hustvedt he gets stuck somewhere. Although he has many female readers and followers, at a certain point he does not go any further, just as Siri Hustvedt's books are read by numerous men, but they apparently cannot draw the right conclusions from it, while women always feel confirmed. They feel it, they look deep into the self-body mirror, but say nothing logically definite about it.

Thus, it becomes clear that it can only be a matter of connecting Φ and Ψ in a suitable way, so that no purely female, no purely male, no somehow imposed or from the outset already definitive, fixed opinion comes into play, but only the human subject itself is made capable of establishing this connection in itself. It's about self-analysis, self-practice. Because once again I can state,

"What there is of the ONE", nobody can convey to another, It, the subject, the ONE, must reveal itself in everyone. For this, however, it may be necessary to give help, nothing more.

Lacan's help is ingenious. He does not assign transcendence, God or anything else to the ONE, but merely says that the psychoanalyst, who has taken the first step into his practice, is ONE for the other who comes in to him, although he is only one among others, as Lacan notes maliciously. He is also the one who thinks he is ONE, although he is two, namely split, and therefore goes into therapy.[49] It goes without saying that Siri Hustvedt doesn't quite get along here, since there are still two for her, the artistic, beautiful, intelligent, if sometimes neurotic woman and the coarse, narrow-minded, sexist man. The father as coordinator does not appear, although you can feel that he is a spiritual statue without signs of too much masculinity. He is almost Ψ, but without Φ. Of course, even Lacan doesn't bring the two together well, even though his work represents the great *Yad'lUn*, from which - if one grasps it so uniformly - Φ/Ψ will be created.

So the help I can give now lies in this formulation, which comes from the Latin language and which I have now presented several times as a formula word (picture above). It consists in the fact that it has no superficial meaning already at hand, but only stimulates

---

[49]Lacan, J., Seminaire XIX, SEUIL (2011) S. 227

the unconscious, even provokes to give out such. The formula-word is language at the edge of the linguistic, i.e. it represents exactly this picture-word-real as it also occurs in the unconscious, even if only purely for the sake of it. In the formula-word, the word is divided into B(r)uchstaben exactly the same as in the unconscious. The meanings in the ENS - CIS - NOM shown above (one can also write it as O.M.E.N.N.S.C.I.S.N or in some other way, whereby the circle writing is the actually important one) thus perfectly represent this linguistic structure, which is at the same time 'crystalline' (Lacan described the unconscious as 'linguistic crystal'). The crystalline is represented by the letter images written in the circle, the linguistic by the multiplicity of meanings. For the meaning of the whole can only consist in animating the unconscious seeing, the image-real as well as the unconscious speaking, the word-real in their commonality, in their successful connection, to awaken themselves, to animate of themselves the film, the text, the *Rays/Speaks* piece, which is the still unconscious identity of the person concerned.

With the formula word E N S - C I S - N O M, the reader only has to sit down and let this formulation, the scientific justification of which I will be supplying shortly, have an effect on him. He can meditate on it in order to experience that here really a subject- and truth-related 'beginning' is found. One has to read it clockwise. In ENS - CIS - NOM the meanings overlap. If one starts once from M above left, then MENS CIS NO means the thinking on this side, within No, starting from N. NOMEN SCIS means, you know the name, OMEN SCIS

N, you know the Omen N, CIS NO, MENS, on this side I swim, oh spirit, ENS CIS NOM, the thing on this side of Nom, C IS NOMEN S, hundred this name S, etc. As nonsensical as some of the meanings may be, they are grammatically and syntactically normal and even semantically ok, but they don't play a role anymore in the further course.

What is important is only the uniform writing like E N S C I S S N O M, which only has to be meditated, mental reverberated, in order to stimulate the unconscious as mentioned. So I let the test persons meditate, but not according to any ideological, neuropsychological, 'spiritual' or purely conventional psychoanalytical guidelines. Everyone can read and study for themselves how the formula words were developed from Lacan's concepts and the meditative process as such (withdrawal from one's own thoughts, e.g. in yoga), how they do not prejudge anything and yet are scientifically structured in the sense of the theory of early body reflections, part one of the method).

The other, second part consists of the fact that the unconscious also contains an It *Speaks*, so that one can also speak with it. Because the unconscious - it is just as crystalline as it is linguistic, linguistically structured - is provoked by a similarly structured, equally structured body of speech, by the mental repetition of a formula word, to give something of its own what I call a password. That's because it brings identity and this is precisely what one has to catch, experience and hear. There is nothing more to be done in the announced procedure of *Analytic Psychocatharsis.*

So the different meanings in practicing this method are too disparate, i.e. cannot be reduced to a common denominator. For if one practices them in the uniform writing, one will never bring the here and now (cis) of Nom with the Omen and the fact that I swim with simultaneous invocation of the spirit (mens) and thereby do my thing (ens) etc. into the ONE of a concept. It is quite clear that it depends in particular on the monotonous repetition of a pure f o r m a l expression and nothing else. One will mentally repeat a kind of nonsense formula, which is not nonsense through lack, but through multiplicity, through the multiplicity of meanings. Freud called this overdetermination as it occurs in dreams, where each element brings together many meanings.

Now it is like this: the sciences that Siri Hustvedt quotes abundantly, further explores and sees through each have their own object that they examine. The atom, biology, the network of the brain. As far as the latter is concerned, I think the splitting into the cerebrum and the mid-brain, the hippocampus, the amygdala and a hundred other areas is sufficient only for network fanatics. The cerebrum (perhaps still with nucleus accumbens and relations to the diencephalon) is responsible for self-refection in the Other and for the thinking of words, the verbal signifiers. The deeper brain regions (interbrain and midbrain with relations to even deeper areas) are responsible for the body's own reflection, for the direct It *Rays* and for the reverberation effects, for the It *Speaks*, which is still immature. Exactly the latter play a role in psychoanalysis, but even more so in *Analytic Psychocatharsis*.

Such a science of the subject, namely, has - as I said - little to do with the brain. Freud and with him Lacan thought that this subject science is about the split human being, which also can be seen in the reflection of the two important brain areas. Because just as the eye cannot see itself in its own core, so one cannot objectify oneself as a subject. René Descartes believed in the well-known sentence of "I think now, therefore I am" that he knew what Siri Hustvedt also criticizes as the Cartesian division of mind and body, and which therefore not sufficient .

Descartes' theorem contains: being because he thinks, and yet he thinks to be, that he thinks, because he is, and so on. Sometimes thinking depends on being, sometimes being depends on thinking. Lacan therefore means that the "subject splits itself from this, that it is at the same time the effect of its mark-up and the support of its deficiency". In other words: by calling itself, thus marking itself, it supports its non-being, because the original being would exist before naming, it thus pulls itself out of the swamp like Baron Münchhausen by its own tuft.

Descartes is the macho scientist who obviously lacks any knowledge of femininity. No woman would think that she is just by thinking, done. But on top of that, Descartes was just with the woman who seemed to present all the women (the universal woman), namely Queen Christina of Sweden (rich, exuberant beauty, educated, regent, etc.), similar to Oedipus with Iocaste, namely, not so good. The queen had invited Descartes to Stockholm to hear about his philosophy. After a few meetings, on a January night in 1650, Descartes had to prove his ability as a lover. Whether he succeeded is not known exactly. In any case, Descartes, who was a notorious late riser, had to leave the royal castle at five o'clock a.m. after an hour of philosophy and love.

After all, no lackey was supposed to watch him leave, and so Descartes stomped his way home at minus temperatures. However, he arrived there very exhausted and fell ill with pneumonia. At that time there was still no penicillin or other macrolides that would have cured the disease quickly, and so the famous philosopher died after a few days in a foreign country. Some political jugglers claimed that there had been arsenic poisoning, because the Swedes feared that Descartes could convert the queen to Catholicism, where her father, Gustav Adolf, was the Protestant leader par excellence. But in reality he died of the woman's weapons, which the Φ of the head-obsessed man - probably through the amorous practical test - unnerved and thus hunted him down.

But with this, Queen Christina has brought herself to the fore as an Φ-oriented power woman and has shown that she perhaps, conversely, does not have enough of Ψ. Siri Hustfeldt would have acted differently there. She at least knows her way around Ψ and knows how to say enough about the hitch and sadness of Φ. Because even if Lacan claims that the feminists deny that Φ is a signifier, something word-real, something verifying and quantifying, this is only half the truth. The whole truth would lie in knowing both symbols, the word-real and the image-real, the It *Speaks* and the It *Rays*, sufficiently well and in addition having found a successful, ideal or at least suitable, happy, scientifically founded combination, knotting (topology!) and interconnection, Φ/Ψ, Body-own / self-in-Other-mirroring

So, Siri Hustfeldts novels and scientifically written essays are not quite enough for such a combination. But I wouldn't know of any other luminous figure of which one could say for sure. The great religious founders, Socrates with his Plato, mystics and philosophers, Freud and Lacan were certainly such luminous beings, but they no longer live, and their works can never completely replace them. So, of course, I myself can't either, I am only the one who developed this cathartic and analytically oriented method, with the help of which I can hope that everyone as an individual, as a bit isolated test person fascinated by the Y a de L'Un, will find the combination mentioned.

Among the great women who have worked on this combination, besides Siri Hustvedt, I would think of Simone de Beauvoir, the life-companion of the philosopher J. P. Sartre. She was very successful with her book 'The Second Sex', but Lacan mocked it and asked what it consisted of: "How can you write about women and call them the second sex? Why not the first gender? Ridiculous! And further: "She [Beauvoir] hated women." Simone de Beauvoir, like her contemporary psychoanalyst J. Kristeva, wrote so many good things about love, but one never knows exactly how to deal with it, because she herself, Beauvoir, doesn't really give the impression that she is a great lover.

She never wanted to be a mother, she never cared about babies.[50] She said that Sartre and herself sufficed each other, which is not true, as everyone now knows. A white coldness and greed for power remained attached to her throughout her life. In the case of the young student B. Lamblin, she even - together with Sartre - endulged in abuse. They both made her their lover, two parental-figures who had a physical relationship with their daughter (Lamblin was many years younger), so to speak.[51] You don't need to be a psychoanalyst to know that all these queer statements about love are very problematic. With Kristeva perhaps, because she enthuses, with Sartre and Beauvoir, because they lie. Siri Hustvedt, however, defends them all.

Simone de Beauvoir was ambitious, she graduated from high school. She was interested in all cultural areas and was one of the committed left-wing social political activists. She always stayed at the Café de Flore, where she met all the interesting intellectuals of Paris at the time, including Sartre. Once she wanted to book a few hours of conversation with Lacan, but he said that just a few hours were not enough. It wouldn't have to be a long psychoanalysis, but forty hours would probably be necessary. But that was too much for Beauvoir again.

---

[50]De Beauvoir, S., In den besten Jahren, Rowohlt (1969) S. 14
[51]Lamblin, B., Memoiren eines enttäuschten Mädchens (Memoirs of a disappointed girl), Rowohlt (1994)

Perhaps there would have been too gross things - not only from her unconscious - but also from the already known personal, delicate relationships brought up.

But perhaps the famous women are not the ones who move the world. Perhaps the majority of women are much more powerful, important and significant in their commitment ('in-between-ness') than we think. Perhaps there is really no such thing as the one who represents all of them, but nevertheless one could erect the theory building of psychoanalysis around them, which in its classical, conventional form revolves around the 'dead father', as has already been suggested several times. He has undoubtedly played a major role in Siri Hustvedt's life, not only because of the trembling he sent her from the realm of the dead. Like Hamlet's father, he appears relatively suddenly as a place to which great distance and remoteness existed, as Siri Hustvedt told of her father. [52]

For her there was the mystery of 'unrecognizability' in him, which frightened her. "My father's unspoken authority was powerful," she writes, which sounds worse than the punishing God of the Old Testament, who at least could be heard. Why didn't she defend herself against him, she wonders, as if there had been an unconscious complicity, a secret that one better didn't even name. But didn't it come up in her psychoanalysis? I can only refer again to Lacan and Judith Le Soldat, who would have drilled into it.

---

[52]Hustvedt, S., Wenn Gefühle auf Worte treffen, Kampa (2019) S. 20 und 34

As a counterweight I want to take now further and in a more decisive form position on women's and queer literature, not only on Siri Hustvedt and S. Beauvoir, but also on all the relationship dramas that permeate the literary market in general. In the past, relationship stories such as M. Mitchell's 'Gone with the Wind', T. Mann's 'Buddenbrooks', Fontane's 'Effi Briest' or Ingeborg Bachmann's 'Works and Letters' were wonderful psychological epics about the relationships of people and especially of the sexes, which seemed grippingly modern compared to Goethe's over-romantized literary style.

But today they seem silly. Today, it is novels like M. Nelson's 'The Argonauts', which are interwoven with transgender layers, that inspire the latest zeitgeist. Whereas M. Mitchell never realized why Scarlett O'Hara passionately admired the completely inconspicuous Ashley, and never came to terms with the grandiose Rhett Butler, M. Nelson is concerned with the lesbian girlfriend who can be transformed into a man while she herself has a child who will be male and thus reflects the same problem - two men and two women. At least that's how the author sees it. Constructive and queer?

But even here and now the so-called 'queer' relationship drama doesn't necessarily work more plausibly than psychology did a hundred years ago. "The literature loves" - so a reviewer about Nelson's book - "the theories, philosophy, submissive sex and faeces."[53] Well, I don't know, apparently it is today, but it sounds a bit steep. There is probably no better way of telling a story than the

[53]Cranach, v, X., literary supplement, SPIEGEL, 30.9.17

other, so that one wonders why literature, despite its considerable walls, will not and probably never succeed in solving the problem of relationship - and above all that of the sexes - well. But let's have a look at women's literature in particular and if they have found out 'What about the ONE'. For it is interesting to search for this superior 'What about the ONE' in all areas (culture, science, art and even literature).

5. Queer and Women's Literature

But before I come to women's literature, I would like to give you a hint about female identity, as it was discovered by psychoanalyst R. Golan. She described the identity of the original female libidinous particularly well. It's about the 'jouissance', which she also calls 'female enjoyment'. This female form of enjoyment - she writes - also "includes pain and suffering, but also includes universality, height, boundlessness, cognition / enlightenment, knowledge, freedom and bliss".[54] Perhaps here we get the answer to the question what autochthonous enjoyment or 'jouissance' per se is, and how man and father, woman and mother share in it.

It doesn't necessarily have to be the intellectual, literarily described and socio-political feminism a la Hustvedt or de Beauvoir, or one of the sadomasochistic visions, as the Christian mystics so well demonstrated when they complained about "the sweet heart pain", like Saint Theresa of Avila for example. The heart, tearing itself apart with longing, always stood in the foreground of religious mysticism. Finally, Saint Theresa quite often saw how "an angel pierced her heart with a lance",[55] which certainly gave rise to erotomaniac interpretations when she explained how this curly, young angel pushed the lance back and forth over and over again.

---

[54]Golan, R. Loving Psychoanalysis, Karnak (2006)
[55]Theresa von Jesu, Die Seelenburg (The castle of soul), Kösel 1973

St. Hildegard von Bingen is also concerned with "building a path from the most intensive of the organism via the elements to the most extreme, the universe",[56] which reminds one of the image-real! Yes, it "arranges all sounding words in itself before it lets them out", which in turn makes one think of the word-reality. She speaks of the "green of the heart's innermost", the viriditas interioris cordis, an elixir that some of our heart patients today could well use!

There is no question that all this sounds like the 'universal women' of that time, i.e. of what a woman was able to achieve at that time beyond being a banal housewife and family. But earlier than today there can be a horror before the reality of the 'jouissance' or the autochthonous enjoyment (as I call it), which is already hinted at in the word 'boundlessness' used by R. Golan above. In addition it is quite helpful to look around in modern, queer women's literatur. Siri Hustvedt's books stand in the foreground, but also other texts by women like V. Woolf, V. Despentes, E. Jelinek, S. Berg and others.

In general, guilt- and shame-complexes appear together, but the main point is that one doesn't have to be ashamed in front of the 'dead father' and one can't be guilty of the universal woman' if you succumb to her. Even if women's literature does not include a theoretisation of the 'universal woman' based on psychoanalysis, in a broader sense female writers are also concerned with this. In one

---

[56]Heidbreder, E., Psychomentaler Stress, Herz - Kreislauf 5 (1984), S. 231

of my earlier books I wrote something about the literature of Virginia Woolf and Virginie Despentes that fits well here. I found it astonishing and curious that the life, desires and writing of the two writers show such unbelievable similarities and at the same time such strong contrasts as one rarely finds, whereby Despentes, with her favouring of drag queens and homosexuality, is to be seen precisely the not yet so well-known sides of this 'universal woman'. In Virginia Woolf's work, on the other hand, this psychological central character wonderfully lets off steam in her lyrical style of writing.

So on the one hand there is this over-sensitive Virginia, who was abused as a teenager by one or even both of her half-brothers, which she did not overcome all her life and commented with the sentence "no longer to be able to enjoy her body any more". She grew up in a well-heeled intellectual milieu and suffered a psychological breakdown at the age of thirteen. On the other hand, one finds this primeval Virginie, who was raped as a youth, but who pushed this event away and repressed it, as she herself says, with male harshness. She grew up in socialist milieu, also had a psychiatric stay when she was fifteen, came into conflict with the police at an early age and agitated against all authorities.

It's funny that they both have virgo, the virgin, in their first names, Virginia Woolf would have liked to remain one, while Virginie Despentes wanted to prove to herself that she never went through such a phase. And while Virginia Woolf marries a man who remains frigid and has a lesbian tendency towards Vita Sackville West, depicting this beloved friend in the novel Orlando as a queer man-woman figure, Virginie Despentes once again has the same and yet completely contradictory relationship. Thus Despentes marries a woman-to-man transsexual, who perhaps - if at all - has had a 'penoid' surgically created with which there could hardly be a satisfying sexuality of which she likes to rhapsodise. She divorced after a few years and then, at the age of thirty-five, also outed herself as a lesbian.

Both women were involved in feminism, with Virginia mainly concerned with equality between men and women, more women's rights through social and literary provocation (especially in her book 'Three Guineas'). She was a co-founder of the Bloomsbury Group of artists and writers. Virginie, on the other hand, tries shocking left-wing and so-called 'pro-sex feminism'. She claims a 'collectively subconscious patriarchy' represses everything sexually feminine, becomes a prostitute for several years, advocates pornography, boasts of contacts with supposedly enthusiastic porn actresses, says that she prefers gay men and that she wants women to be guys and men to be whores and mothers. Well, everything is present - almost some queerness.

After all, the same phenomenon of similarity and divergence between the two women can also be found in literature. V. Woolf writes in her book 'The Waves' about six protagonists (three male, three female) in an almost lyrical form, in which the voices, statements and self-talks of these six persons occur mainly. "I love, Susan said, and I hate. . . My eyes are hard. Jinnys eyes spray in a thousand lights. Rhoda's eyes are like the pale blossoms the moths come to in the evening. . . But when we sit close together, Bernard said, we melt together in phrases. We are surrounded by haze. We form an intangible area. . . and much later] . . A good phrase seems to me to have an independent existence. But I believe that the best ones probably come about in loneliness."[57]

The fact that good phrases have an independent existence could come from Lacan, in whom the word-real dominates psychoanalysis. And if it's good, this word-real, it's because it also carries with it the image-real that was standard with Virginia Woolf. Her metaphors are constantly interspersed with nature-animal-landscape-light-smiles and similar allegories, and as just shown, it is primarily the words, the sentences, the linguistic rhythms that live here, which equally ideally depict the female libido waves. In her book 'Woolf mit Lacan', the research assistant for women's studies at the University of Bielefeld, Germany, establishes a connection between the texts in the book 'The Waves' and Lacan's psycho-analysis.[58] It shows how the characters in the novel are constituted by speaking and how ego education and libido condition and prevent each other.

According to Lacan, libido is an organ that exists only as a pure 'life instinct', i.e. it is not biological, which is why in Woolf's novels it can become extremely alive purely through 'phrases'. Everything exists through the

---

[57]Woolf, V., Die Wellen (The waves), Suhrkamp (1964) S. 15, in my text everything is back-translated
[58]Müller, M., Woolf mit Lacan, Der Signifikant in den Wellen (the signifier in the waves), Aisthesis Verlag (1993)

wonderful word, through the play between identity and difference, self-dissolution and significant ego-being. Virginia's libido is 'desexualized' as Freud called it, she closes the circle in the woman's body, not constantly pushing herself outwards, as is usually the case with men. Virginia would almost be the 'universal woman' if she had understood how to play out her wealth libidinously.

In Despentes, on the other hand, the organ libido is conjured up biologically and bodily up to the maximum, it is celebrated in her books through sex and porn, through male aggressiveness and female thinking. In her more recent books, the author increasingly deals with the social peripheries, the marginalized, those destroyed by state-based lack of understanding and individuals fighting wildly for their sexual identities in dramatic form. In doing so, she manages to reach a key as rhythmic as the one I emphasized in Virginia Woolf, even though it sounds much more vulgar. She cannot be a poet like Virginia Woolf, she writes journalistically. She does not celebrate the tender souls, but writes of the 'subconscious' (not of the unconscious, as the usage of language provides, but of the spiritual 'bottom'), of the perverse.

Seen this way, I can draw a conclusion: both women are still in the immature structure of an unconscious position, that is to say, my esteemed own mirroring and echo reverberating, both in Spiritual-Literary in Virginia and in Literary-Obscene in Virginie. Woolf goes too far into the overflowing fantasies and self-talks, which she herself followed and which her protagonists follow intensively in the book 'The Waves'. She is too much in the mirror-others and - as already emphasized - in the phrases. Three hundred pages of sun, wind, the lisp of the leaves, the tumult of love and the rustle of the woods are piled up in excessively lengthy sentences. Despentes, on the other hand, hopes that through their pithy descriptions of abysmal sex and social descent, the subjects will allow themselves to be drawn into their discourse, in other words into the bright light of the body's own mirror and the loud call of echo reverberation. In the latest book 'Vernon Subutex' this consists of a staccato and a suada of vulgar and faecal language, of drugs, perversion and pornography.

Both writers lack the possibility for the human subject participating in the lives of these women to find its own, perhaps libidinous-literary, with which the unconscious positions can be further overcome. Of course, both writers have found a kind of counter language to everyday normality, in which everything comes across more authentic, contrapuntal and plastic, and a quite original *Rays / Speaks* emerges. What I could see in the biographical material, both had bad relations to their mothers. As in the reversed Oedipus complex, the desire to recognize the highly stylized father and the hatred for the mothers, who do not satisfy the two women's excessive claim to love, play a decisive role in the soul complex.

They are in a vehement struggle for identity with the 'universal woman'. But the intellectual or socialist and libidinously 'castrated' father - so to speak 'dead father' - is loved. Castrated' because both women could hardly have imagined the father as a sexually active man, but as a bohemian statue, as a friendly interlocutor, as an asexual figure, as a hero en titre, they could appreciate him. Maybe Siri Hustvedt's problem lies here as well, namely that her father, as a professor of Norwegian and American history, was a respected and dignified, stately figure, but he nevertheless concealed something libidinous that seemed ominous. But you can hide the ominous, and then the father appears glorified like a stylized statue.

Thus the depiction of the two women writers I have just portrayed also runs through the seemingly insurmountable splitting that I have mentioned several times and that I consider so essential - purely formal, purely primary mirror-like and echo-logic, "crystalline-linguistic". And at the same time I would like to use it in the form of *Rays / Speaks* with the method of *Analytic Psychocatharsis*. The 'jouissance feminine', the autochthonous enjoyment, wasted itself in Woolf's love of art, culture, literature and the afterlife, while Verginie Despentes doesn't even know it exists. On the other hand, she relies on gender relations, of which Lacan says on every third page of his work that - as has already been hinted at several times above - it is not logically speakable, nor definitively expressible nor writeable and so actually does not exist.[59]

---

[59]V. Despentes is right when she says that we are repressing everything, especially what she shows. But there is also a 'successful repression' in psychoanalysis, a kind of healthy forgetting. I, for example, don't want to be reminded of the disgraceful deeds of my younger days, I'm glad to have

Behind Verginie Despentes horny porn language, however, one suspects on the one hand the longing for intact, rich, intensive and yet also harmonious relationships, for loving family, which also applies to Virginia Woolf, but on the other hand also the hunch that there must be something like an autochthonous enjoyment that could compensate for the lack of external relationships. According to Virginie Despentes, one only has to penetrate deeper, more extreme and more violent into lewd maximal eroticism in order to get to the very last of these drinking, smoking, anarchy and sexual pleasures, and where should one break through with it, if not on the back and opposite side of the same medal, where the most lovely magic, the aura of Virginia Woolf's most heavenly spirit, thrones deliriously in her metaphors.[60] Really, they're both queer.

The medal consists of an overly strong longing for melting love, which is why autochthonous enjoyment is missed. Because this is already love in itself, love for itself as another, complete and yet stripped of make-up, detached love. Romantic love is a comedy, judges Lacan rightly. Mother-child love is the most valuable of the early years of life, if it is too cool or if it cools down too quickly, it is sad. If this early love was and remains

processed them. So why should I read more than a few pages of 'Vernon Subutex'? Everything is already ticked off.

[60]Also here: why should I read it more than once when it does not sound like Goethe's 'Wilhelm Meisters Wanderjahre' like 'a highly tired, dignified sclerotic conglomeration', as Thomas Mann said in this regard, but is still abundantly elegiac-delivering and supra-aesthetic.

overprotective even later, one becomes neurotic. The most impressive brave-child story is about the doctor J. Haarer, who wrote the book 'The German Mother and her first Child' in 1934, which was a huge success, and who in an interview with her youngest daughter G. Haarer wrote 'The German Mother and her last Child' in response. In the Zeit magazine of 19 September 2019, A. Kemper describes how the relationship between these two women is superimposed by Nazi ideology, permeated by female ambition and the will to survive, dead silence, coldness, suicide of the husband or rather father, a difficult literary legacy and finally animated by the love of this daughter, wandering through all the psychological categories.[61] Moving, strong.

All this does not exist in Sybille Berg's latest book GRM, Brainfuck, in which even the title is inteded to sound provocative. In the ZEIT from 18. 4. 2019, literary critic U. March writes that "the story of four children from the lower classes, who all suffer from ADHD, autism and the violence inflicted on them, is not only one of the best, but also one of the worst that contemporary German-language literature has to offer. . . When her mountain machete assassins tells of, embryos torn from their wombs, sex slaves and gangs of rapists in a world in which the British economy is dominated by Chinese companies and in which people are monitored

---

[61]Kemper, A., Interview mit G. Haarer, im Zeit-Magazin, Nr. 39 (2019)

everywhere, the critic recognises, despite all the 'monstrosity', the contemporary".[62]

Contemporary reference? It's only queerness. The horrors of the Second World War weren't bad either, and aren't they still relevant to the present or have we just forgotten them again? And medieval times have similar things to offer, and yet Sybille Berg is full of Queerness, who is strangely often portrayed as such a sexist raging maenad, although she can also be Madame, virtuoso and goddess. It's hard to say what it's all about, the image-real trumps the word-real to such an extent that there's no connection between the two anymore. The newspaper DIE WELT, on the other hand, writes about the author's book: "The whole thing is so gloomy that the reviewer asks herself at the end who would want to read it voluntarily. We want to learn the 'jouissance' from the women and not the sounds of murder, right? No, both are necessary.

Among the writers of the twentieth century there are many more to mention who, in addition to their literary abilities, were cult figures of a sort, mundanities, excitement or social peculiarities and queer fighters. One could easily mention George Sand, Jane Austen, Emelie and Charlotte Bronte, the Reventlow, Susan Sontag, Ingeborg Bachmann and numerous other authors to make it clear how close they came to the 'universal woman'. The most accurate and queer, however, seems to me to be Nobel laureate Elfriede Jelinek, whose range of bourgeois abilities on the one hand and emancipatory

---

[62] März, U., Ein Buch wie ein Sprengsatz (A book like an explosive device), ZEIT online, 18.4.19

gain on the other is enormous. Her mother belonged to the upper middle classes, her father, a so-called 'Halbjude', had to endure many problems in the Third Reich and was already mentally seriously disturbed in Elfriede Jelinek's childhood years.

While she herself grew up in a Catholic kindergarten and then in a monastery school, she also learned to play musical instruments at an early age and received appropriate training. However, she also fell mentally ill and joined Prof. Asperger at the Vienna University Hospital. Asperger was not only the first to describe the form of autism named after him, he is also said to have referred children to the institution 'Am Spiegelgrund', where child euthanasia was practised. So it was certainly not so great to be there. Elfriede Jelinek studied art history, but had to interrupt it, because of an anxiety disorder. Only after her father's death at the end of the sixties and with her participation in the 68 revolt did she - as they say - find herself.

Now she joined the Communist Party of Austria and wrote her first books, the Marxist-Feminist novel 'die liebhaberinnen' (the mistresses of love). With the works 'Die Klavierspielerin' (the female pianist) and 'Lust' she became a stylised female 'pornographer' and remained the agonist against Austria's Nazi repression machinery. All the more surprising that she was awarded the Nobel Prize for Literature in 2004, which triggered protests worldwide and made it impossible for her to receive this prize personally in Stockholm. But there was probably also an inhibition on her part to have to face the venerable old gentlemen of the Nobel Prize Committee and to give a tight speech without solid vocabulary in front of numerous international guests. The 'universal woman' would have caused a scandal that would have made her poor and a 'notorious heretic' (punished like Jeanne D'Arc).

The following comment can be read in the ZEIT online from 4. 11. 83:[63] *Not only since her latest novel "The female pianist", the vivisection of a mother-daughter relationship and at the same time the story of the destruction of female sexuality, the 37-year-old Viennese author has been regarded as a hate specialist.. Even the extremism of the depictions and the bawdiness of the language - which men such as Heiner Müller, Henry Miller or Jean Genet are easily granted - cannot be tolerated with Mrs. Jelinek.*

"At some point I no longer write, but it begins to write me," says Jelinek. Writing as self-therapy, writing as a substitute for psychotherapy. "Actually, I was always in treatment. I had a total of four psychiatrists. I was an only child under extremely strained family circumstances, from the pathology of my father and from the bad marriage of my parents". . The father had been a scattered genius, belonging to "the Slavic-depressive Jewish culture". He died in spiritual disarray, "the most tragic being I have ever met," and left his daughter a lifelong fear of madness as the close and terribly familiar.
. . .

---

[63]Löffler, S., Spezialistin für den Hass (specialist for hate) , ZEIT online, 4. 11. 83

She had been trained by her mother to become a clever child prodigy, had learned to dance ballet and walk almost simultaneously at the age of two or three, had started studying the violin at the age of eight and the organ at the age of thirteen. . . She was educated in the consciousness of the unusual and exclusive. She felt . . . of the practical ability to live of her mother as if slain. When she was eighteen, she collapsed and could not leave the house for a year because of fear: "I was in a terrible state. I was really totally broken. . . . "

Elfriede Jelinek, communist and mundane lady too at the same time, thus represents a woman with a large span, with enormous complexity and versatility, she challenges anyone, man or woman. She awakens, polarizes and gives suggestions to all possible areas of life, cultural, scientific, general. And above all: she gives reason to be ashamed, if one disfigures the woman in such a way (e.g. as fully veiled or only as housewife at the stove), abuses (e.g. as sexual object or showgirl), exploits (as inferior in badly paid occupations, etc.). Maybe Elfriede Jelinek first saw her father positively and then had to experience his fall, while at the same time the mother stood above her as an unapproachable icon. Anyway, as little as we don't have to get along with the 'dead father', the 'proper name', the alpha and omega and work through our guilt complexes on him, so much do we need the figure, the body mirror, the mythical universality of the 'universal woman' to experience and cope with our shame complexes.

We need women's literature, for Goethe can no longer help us, who at the end of his 'Faust'   described the "eternally feminine" as that which "hinanzieht" (attracts up), i.e. what drags to and pulls up, which does not sound as only uplifting as he and many others have meant to him. So female enjoyment is not so much the abreaction of a pleasure where one is only attracted to and attracted up, and it is also difficult to say where and how it is realized in different ways. Let me remind you once again that Lacan always emphasised how little women appreciate and tend to disregard this enjoyment of their own. They feel it, but perhaps they don't know how to say it definitively or logically, and so their enjoyment usually falls by the wayside, even if, in addition to the modern writings, the outpourings of a Mechthild of Magdeburg or Saint Theresa of Avila and a few others undoubtedly have a meaning in terms of 'jouissance'.

6. Matriarchy and Separation Rage

Why is conventional psychoanalysis so cumbersome, why must one first bring along a positive transfer, which is then dissolved again by the therapist's interpretations because of its inadequate contents? Why can't certain aspects of this transmission be allowed to exist, since it has a close relationship to sublimation, self-upliftment, refinement, which works like an independent drive? The philosopher and sociologist T. Lipowatz, in his book 'The Denial of the Political', very nicely emphasized that the path of human progress "can reopen within the framework of discrete brotherhood in psychoanalysis", which "means for the subject that its truth does not appear only at the end of the process, as with Hegel or Marx, but on the way, in surprise, at the edges, beside it ... ".[64] He also said that individuation (self-discovery) and love for transcendence are the two main pillars of life.[65]

Transfer, which is also referred to as love of transfering, is not so far away from transcendence and a love for it, but for classical psychoanalysts this sounds too much like a detached myth, something spiritual. However, in the end it's just psychoanalysis a little bit different. Because

---

[64]Lipowatz,T., Die Verleugnung des Politischen (The Denial of the Political), Quadriga (1986) S. 220
[65]Lipowatz T., Der Fortschritt der Geistigkeit und der Tod Gottes (The Progress of Spirituality and the Death of God), Königshausen & Neumann (2005)

the causality principle (the unconscious desire is the cause for the symptoms) can also be contrasted with a final principle (psychoanalysts like S. Leikert and R. Zwiebel have worked out this aspect).[66] Both speak of the unconscious, the rhythmic, which contains 'tonality', the visual, the pictorial and the creative. They emphasize the more meditative and cathartic side, which should be considered more extensively in today's psychoanalysis.[67] In any case, something exists here that has been neglected in Freudian psychoanalysis and its emphasis on the lexical, verbal language, and so they also want to put the image-real and the reflections, the mirrorings in the foreground.

I also try this in *Analytic Psychocatharsis*, even if here I am not leaning on a love for transcendence, but on a love for this connection of the word-real and image-real, for the formula-like names. "Love", says Lacan somewhere in relation to what has been said so far, "only exists for one name". Love for people and for things has only a limited value. But a name not only confirms what it expresses, but also leads beyond it into 'in-between-ness', into the world of bridging from radiance to speech and vice versa, to "a love for oneself that makes you happy", as the title of the last book of the psychoanalyst M.

---

[66]Leikert, S., Schönheit und Konflikt, Umrisse einer allgemeinen psychoanalytischen Ästhetik (Beauty and Conflict,Outlines of psychoanalytic Ästhetics) , Psychosozial Verlag (2012).

[67]Zwiebel, R., Weischede, G., Neurose und Erleuchtung, Klett-Cotta (2009)

Mitscherlich called it.[68] That sounds a bit narcissistic. She would perhaps have written better: "A love for oneself as Other ..." or "A love for her own unconscious" than the still unfinished and yet promising.

Mitscherlich did not mean a vain self-love, she was more concerned with the love for her conversations with her patients, which she could still have at an advanced age, where it is about love, about the act of love, which is realized through patient listening and interpretations. The statements of the pass words in *Analytic Psychocatharsis* are also not narcissistic, they do not support vain self-love. And also the love of the therapist is not in demand.

What would that mean if the therapist loved his patients directly? Nothing at all. It must be about a "detached love",[69] which the translator of this psychoanalytic article in German translated as "separated love". I would rather speak of a disengaged, respectful love, of a love that works from the background, from a slight distance, by not imposing itself and not revealing itself as such. But this is exactly what makes it more effective than anything else. Now one only has to turn the whole into the "detached love", which lies in the process of meditation, *Analytic Psychocatharsis* itself, because it is scientifically founded, and this way turns into a love for science, too.

---

[68]Mitscherlich, M., Eine Liebe zu sich selbst, die glücklich macht (A love for oneself that makes one happy), S. Fischer (2013)

[69]Kohon, G., Love in a time of madness. In Green & Kohon: Love and its vicissitudes, Routledge (2005) p. 41 - 100

This may sound too sober, not queer enough, but I have stressed several times that it is a science of the subject, a conjectural science, not a cold intelligence or technique as they are otherwise customary in the sciences.[70] There is enough queer literature in this respect, for example with Shakespeare's Hamlet, who Tennyson described as "the greatest of all literary works," because it's about love, death, and everything else. Hamlet never existed, even if the story is based on a historically real pre-version of the early Middle Ages. But Hamlet's name is a symbol for a special radiance, for a literary singularity. For Hamlet is not himself.

He is the absolute son, the "fils-père" as the French say, the father-son, who does not live his own time and identity, but that of his producer. It is impossible to see why he has to rage so hard against his mother and his uncle. It is said that the father died in "his sins bloom", killed by his own brother, who then immediately married Hamlet's mother. This sounds like a plot, of course, and Hamlet's father suggests this to him as a ghost from the realm of the dead. But it could well be that one had to more or less rightly eliminate the old ruler, who was obviously guilty of error and sin, because otherwise the state could have perished.

But psychologically it is clear that Hamlet resembles Oedipus very much. So it is clear that Hamlet's mother

---

[70]Conjecture means assumption, which - as already Nikolaus von Cues stated in his writing 'de conjectura' - through further assumptions becomes more and more condensed into something true, until a final conclusion is certain.

Gertrude had a love relationship with Claudius, the brother of her husband, and Claudius killed his brother out of greed for power and jealousy, who then (classic case of the 'dead father') appeared to his son as a ghost to the dead and called him to revenge. In fact, Hamlet's relationship with his mother is marked by an intimacy of his own, he hesitates forever to kill his uncle. Gertrude fits well as a queen, femme fatal, player for power, lover, as the 'universal woman'.

Hamlet was presented in increasingly grotesque forms as being schizotypically disturbed in his personality, that, according to Goethe, he was "ailing from the paleness of thought", so weak, bloodless, introverted. But in reality he pulls his thing through to the end. Even before he purposefully completes his work by killing his uncle, he stabs Polonius, Ophelia's father, impulsively from behind a wallpaper. Hamlet has not only been compared with Oedipus by Freud, but also by many commentators, although the events almost look like an exchange of roles, i.e. upside down.

But in a nutshell, all the descriptions can be traced back to the Oedipal conflict, Now revenge is actually only the reversal of guilt. By wanting to kill his father's brother, Hamlet eliminates the man next to his mother, next to whom he could have stood as king himself, like the unconsciously incestuous Oedipus who stands next to Iocaste. To kill the uncle and stepfather, Hamlet is made guilty, who is only in a narrow sense a good father's son, who still obeys the father in his abstract form as a ghost. But especially the brave father-sons secretly concoct the worst patricides. Thus Oedipus is also a particularly considerate, thoughtful type who left his foster father Polybos in Corinth in order not to be tempted to kill him - as prophesied by the oracle. But with that he just came close to his real father and his atrocity.

But as far as love is concerned, especially 'detached love', Shakespeare's 'King Lear' can be better adhered to. In this drama the two older daughters only pretend to love the domineering and authoritative king, only play as he imagines it: theatrically, affectively, loudly. Cordelia, the youngest daughter, on the other hand, clearly says that she "loves him out of duty". But King Lear misunderstands this utterance, he understands it as many would otherwise do, namely as coercion, as a rule, as actually a loveless motto. In reality, however, Cordelia's love is exactly that of the 'detached mood', of the serious, silent, true love, the only type that can change something. Exactly this love is the type that matters, because it is the love of the proper name, the name that really describes what being a king means, and with which Cordelia wants to bring her father to his senses, to salvation, to truth.

In his book 'The Fatherless Society', A. Mitscherlich showed that we all - even if not directly and real - reject the actual fathers. We disregard them because they are sometimes overly strict, bizarre and selfish, but to wipe them out completely humiliates you. Lacan wasn't a patricide, but he once told his training analyst that he had just taken a truck's right of way with his little Citroën 2CV on the way to him. So he alluded to little Oedipus, who wants to show his father who comes first and is stronger. And the one (Löwenstein, Lacan's teaching analyst) actually allowed to be put on by not recognizing the allusion to the father/son conflict and saying nothing about it. Had he not noticed the parallelism to the Oedipus conflict, or had he recognized the allusion and evaluated it too playfully?

Similarly, it was only the other way round when, after thirty hours of teaching analysis, I told my teaching analyst that I was well enough analysed and trained. He too should have interpreted it as an evil act of mine to dethrone him from his legal pedestal like Oedipus did. But he only soberly referred to a somewhat institutionally higher number of hours, and I recognized my patricidal intention myself much later. Obviously I wanted to get to paradise called psychoanalysis much earlier than it would have been good, where one tries to speak the language without words (without fixed vocabulary), the female language (of listening, of consideration).

The author T. Meinecke, who describes himself as a Feminist and follower of 'female writing', tries something like this in accordance with the previous chapter on women's literature.[71] But the matter quickly becomes clear, Meinecke believes that he can forget the man if he writes feministically and emphasises that not the physiological does determine gender, but the social. But he confuses the social with the unconscious and refers to 'gender studies' of feminist philosopher Judith Butler. Now the psychoanalyst and matriarchal researcher E. Bornemann tried the same thing forty years ago. He wrote: "As a man, why do I write such a primer that gives

---

[71]Interview in the SZ from 16. 5. 2029, p. 17 with the title: Sexuality is still a prison.

women the arguments to overthrow their own sex? [72] That sounds tricky, of course. For like Meinecke, he believed that in using such argumentation he would be recognized as what he wanted to be: a scientist, a man who must be taken seriously as a man. If you write 'feminine', if you dress up as a feminist, so the motto, then you are off the hook, then you are confirmed as a feminist. But true feminists don't take that from anyone.

All this reminds one a bit of so-called matricentric societies (allegedly a better expression than matriarchal), where conversely to the just mentioned men in disguise, "the woman was prophetess, priestess, judge, doctor, queen and goddess". [73] The latter was perhaps too much of a good thing, because in the so-called patriarchate, men were never God themselves, they had skilfully transported Him to afterlife and could thus remain Andriarchates, male rulers. And also, matricentric societies were probably no "love cultures par excellence, in which there were no contradictions to be solved aggressively, for ... the male principle was completely embedded in a female universe," [74] the author boldly claims.

---

[72]Bornemann, E., Das Patriarchat. Ursprung und Zukunft un-seres Gesellschaftssystems (The Patriarchate. Origin and Future of Our Social System), S. Fischer ()1975
[73]Gould-Davis, E., Am Anfang war die Frau (In the Beginning Was The Woman), München (1977) S. 346
[74]Göttner - Abendroth, H., Die Göttin und ihr Heros, Verlag Frauenoffensive (1980) S. 6

In her multi-volume work "The Matriarchy" Göttner-Abendroth turns primarily against the research into matriarchy that had arisen through male prejudices, which even often claims that there had never been anything like a long lasting epoch of matriarchal cultures.[75] And she also turns against the last pivot of some matriarchal researchers, namely by pull herself out of the affair by a kind of self-accusation, as just quoted by Bornemann. Such an approach - to offer women the opportunity to sacrifice masculinity in order to assert themselves as scientists - sees through Göttner-Abendroth and wants an "autonomous formulation in their world view of feminine and historical interpretation". This can be understood. But when Göttner-Abendroth puts the word "autonomous" in this place, it is no less delicate. If as a man he makes unproven assertions, the woman naturally feels threatened in her autonomy, but does she not perhaps have the word autonomy from him? From him when he tries to be scientific?

Especially in such early social societies, as for example the Himbas in today's Namibia are, strict, affect-regulating procedures apply. The ethnopsychoanalysis by A. Köhler-Weisker also showed this with this people.[76]

---

[75]Göttner - Abendroth, ., Das Matriarchat, Bd. I, Kohlhammer (1988)

[76]Köhler - Weisker, A., Gespräche unter dem Mopanebaum, Ethnopsychoanalytische Begegnungen mit den Himba-nomaden (conversations under the mopane tree, ethnopsychoanalytical encounters with the Himbanomades), psycho-sozial-Verlag (2015)

During her long conversations with a young Himba woman, the analyst comes across homoeroticism in the form of countertransference, in which she herself develops feelings for her graceful body and her natural movements and emotions. The whole thing becomes a latent to semi-manifest homophilia, which is not lived out, but clearly in play. It represents the self-element that enables the entry into ethnopsychoanalysis both affectively and interpre-tatively.

Weisker-Köhler sometimes poses the wrong questions when she addresses her analysand with very individual feelings. Similar to many primary peoples, e.g. the Iatmul, such emotions are also taboo with the Himbas or are only experienced very shamefully, so that one cannot and does not want to talk about them. Nevertheless, the author discusses the aspect of an 'in-between corporeality', which is supposed to go beyond the usual purely social inter-subjectivity and which one would have to transculturally develop in order - in my language - to bring the image-word reality into play. The author also believes that the reality of the ultimate separation can be bridged by the 'mutual internalization process' in which the Western woman was able to experience her latent homoeroticism and an almost family connection with the Himbas' body-near and less pronounced demarcations between them.

She can work out the repressed 'separation rage' of the Himba women, who mourn only weakly the abandonment of parents and life partners and are not allowed to shout out their rage and anger about it. Such a thing could also be helpful for us, because even in our society the individual is not always aware of how often he is actually angry about separations. The Himba women compensate the lacking separation processing by relationship with a lover, when the men graze the cattle herds long time and far away. This false adultery is socially sanctioned, even if the lover is not allowed to be caught directly. So he must behave as Descartes had to do with Queen Christina, namely disappear from the love nest before dawn.

For Kybele, the matriarchal goddess, was able to enchant the men so much that they enthusiastically made themselves their eunuch priests. But today we know that this was supposed to be a symbolic death. Couldn't it be otherwise? For example, in a psychoanalysis to pronounce yourself in such a way that nothing remains of one? Because that's all they missed in matriarchy: they didn't take dying seriously. They didn't take death as real. The children who were sacrificed to Baal, the young men who emasculate before Kali, they do it paranoid 'voluntarily', in divine ecstasy. Exactly, the whole thing is an alleged "natural sex", and in it everything merges. Undoubtedly this is no different in the Andriarchates, which unfortunately are always called Patriarchates. Here the slaughter is perfectly planned for political reasons and carried out in wars.

I'm writing all this to show again that nowhere is 'What about the ONE' realized. Nobody goes deep into themselves, nobody works with the early body-own mirrorings and their connection with the echo effects.

They all go outside first and try some tricks. The same goes for the transgender people who don't see their most original being. As Meinecke and Bornemann try to become scientists by 'female or feminist crying' from men, so the transgender people see themselves as the sex they were born with as not confirming enough. They think that they get the recognition in the other gender: but now quite normal, so to speak state-recognized, according to the norm, but just different. Differently normal, with the emphasis on normal. The same goes for the above-mentioned men, who also want to be normal scientists, because they feel that the way they did science left them with only abnormal men, whose preference for football, fast cars and sex they reject.

And that, this 'the other way round normality', is what Hamlet also wants. He is not the sick man, but the mad normal man, because his tricks - with which, for example, he shows his uncle Claudius a theater showing the same murder method with which Claudius killed Hamlet's father without leaving a trace - are ingeniously normal. No real madman could act as skilfully as Hamlet snubs Ophelia, sends his childhood friends to their doom and finally stabs Claudius. And so we continue the word Hamlet, the name Hamlet, Hamlet as an image-word real, because he can make us believe that it tells us a lot, when it should be about nothing, which is only a breath, a dot of language, an oracle, a piece of phrase, a psst! a wow! an emoji. Because even the letters H.a.m.l.e.t are too much to find 'what about ONE.'.

For it is a name fixed to its complex, while only the name is helpful, which says nothing, which has not already determined everything from the beginning. Password and formula word are also names, but they are not presumptive, not preconceived. Where the formula word contains several preconceived meanings, it does not result in a uniformly fixed meaning. The password word, on the other hand, seems to contain something preconceived, but it concerns exactly that, whose preconception, its fixed truth, one wants to know, because it is supposed to express one's own, 'What about the ONE'. The experience of the password may seem like an almost audible thought coming from afar or from depth. In any case, it is clearly delimitable and can usually be grasped rationally like. The best way to explain this is to give another example.

One of my patients, for example, who had been using the analytic psychocathartic method for some time, had suddenly grasped the thought or 'heard' it in the background while practicing: "Not self latticed". As strange as this thought was, it was equally clear to her. It concerned her professional and private life situation, in which she felt locked up, "latticed or barred". Now it is perhaps not a great idea that one is "latticed" in one's life situation, because somehow one does not get ahead and blocks everything. But when one experiences this thought from the unconscious, from one's own inner being, even like an echo in one's own body, this is something different. It has an important character as a well-intentioned advice, even as an admonition from the outside not to allow oneself to be so constricted or barred. But through a phrase that points out: "don't lattice yourself", but also: "it's not you who bars or lattices yourself", the matter gets more substance, especially by questioning the password a little rationally.

So there is a big difference when you say to yourself in a sober everyday condition that you are somehow locked up and have to free yourself from it or also when acquaintances or friends mediate this. You already know that and take it to heart. But the fact that there is something here that can speak to the other person per se is much more impressive. It works like a metaphysical advice, like a revelation, like a perfect interpretation of transference, about which one can think and orientate oneself for a long time.

"To bar, to lattice" also has a somewhat different meaning than being imprisoned or repressed, as one would most likely consciously think. The unconscious speaks quite drastically, provokingly and revealingly also in the dream or in the slip of the tongue. The fact that one can be "latticed" is not such a common expression and reminded the patient that her family often seemed quite "latticed" to her. But there was also the thought of being "behind bars", which added to the drama, because the patient had also associated that her father had been "behind bars" for a short time when she was very young.

And indeed, in another conversation it came out that these never processed events were possibly a reason for her own "being imprisoned in herself" - as she continued to express it. She had suffered for years from the fact that her father "was a criminal", although he was only imprisoned for a shorter period for a financial crime that was not committed alone by him and not very significant.

It was not only he himself who had been 'barred' here, because after more than he had been found guilty a colleague in the same matter. But this had never been fully explained to her, and it had become 'latticed' in her, because she had felt preferred to her mother's father, which now seemed to be destroyed and which at the same time represented an oedipal problem.

To become clear about all this helped her decisively. So it can also be understood why I call such an 'ultra-reduced phrase' a pass-word, an identity word. It gives an indication of one's own identity, adds a new aspect or, as in classical psychoanalysis, creates an insight into the essence of identity. But this insight is much more direct and subject-related. Such insights are not always easy to cope with, but when one hears it from oneself, it is much more familiar and personal and thus easier to integrate. And it also works more definitive, because it comes from oneself, from a very deep layer, that of the autochthonous, which must be opened and liberated for enjoyment.

Exactly for this reason we are dealing here with 'What about the ONE', with Krause's 'interconnection of the two 'organisation cores' (*Rays / Speaks*), which everyone can only complete as an individual. He can accomplish it more often, because of the pass-words one can have also several, as I will describe in later chapters.

7. Memories of the Future

Fortunately, Siri Hustvedt has published another novel - entitled 'Damals' (Memories of the Future) - which peppered with many neuroscientific and psychological aspects fits well into my book again. But maybe it's not so happy, because Siri Hustvest's book contains a lot of things she has described before: about artistically gifted and neurotic women and about bad and sexist men, whereby in the main character of the book with the acronym H. H. the author hides herself again. It is about her childhood and youth years until today, and the text is undoubtedly fluent and easy to read again.

Now I'm not doing anything else. All my books deal with the method of *Analytic Psychocatharsis*, what it is and how to use it. But because I can already explain this on a few pages (see appendix), my writing would have become very boring. So I have done it with stories from different sciences, from reports about society and culture and from the psychoanalysis of Lacan. For the constant repetition and the same outcome, the same conclusion, I am therefore sometimes mocked. Well, one can endure that and Siri Hustvedt will also have endured some harsh criticism of her books with always similar contents.

In the online edition of the ZEIT the literary critic U. March writes that the American author Siri Hustvedt is a literary star whose celebrity has gone to her head. "According to Siri Hustvedt, she has had enough of private anecdotes (her marriage to P. Auster, etc.), and it is true, of course, that they have nothing to do with the aesthetic rank of her work, strictly puristically speaking. It is also true, however, that the communicative space that literature occupies has never been solely due to printed words, but also to its "round-about it", its social spectacle including celebrities. And stars like Siri Hustvedt fill theatre halls. To dismiss this as an entertainment event would be a mistake. The star appearance represents literature as a mobilizing event, the numbers of visitors to the Leipzig Book Fair and the lit. Cologne speak for themselves. And this representation ultimately benefits one of every reading in the library room".[77]

In the abridged version of U. März's review of the aforementioned book, the criticism that I just mentioned above comes to light: " Her new novel 'Damals' (Memories of the Future) is an annoying celebration of platitudes and know-it-all. Ursula März thinks Siri Hustvedt's new novel is a soap bubble. She has to read a lot of 'trivial Freudianism' and a lot of clichés about sexist men in the story of a young woman in New York in the late 70s who resembles the author's hair, but then again not. Above all, the gesture of knowing what's going on and the unrestrained educational hypocrisy in the text are a brutal nuisance for März, not least because the author has nothing new to add to the 20th century memory literature. With all due respect for Hustvedt's 'text-theoretical' ambitions, the book is above all sententious

---

[77]März, U., Ein weiblicher Narzissmus (A female narcissism), DIE ZEIT vom 12. 4. 2019 und ein Kommentar in Perlentaucher online.

and a little clumsy for the reviewer. It is the hot air of a specially female narcissism".

The commentary in the FAZ of March 22, 2019, is quite different: "Reviewer Verena Lueken has been abducted by Siri Hustvedt into the wonderful realm of fiction, in which 'knowledge, experience, choice and feeling' become one. She follows the writer in admiration as she remembers the young woman who came to New York in 1978 to conquer the future at the age of sixty. Lueken likes Hustvedt's play with identities, with role assignments and reflections, she effortlessly follows the various narrative strands and levels and in between changes to Hustvedt's essays, in which she finds the same reflection on false juxtapositions - content and form, feeling and reason, body and soul, man and woman - as in these "memories of the future of yore".[78]

What is it about Siri Hustvedt that is really true? It's true that she's pulling out her old stops again, yet the subject she raises, the subject of man and woman, is vital for all people today, even if Siri Hustvedt can't find a real solution. The picture on the cover of 'Damals' was drawn by herself and probably shows her as a naked woman who floats over the Empire State Build-ing with her arms outstretched, holding a knife in her right hand. Those who know her story know that this knife saved her from rape in her youth.

---

[78]Lueken, V., Ein Portrait der Künstlerin als junge Frau, FAZ vom 22. 3. 2019 und Kommentar in Perlentaucher online

She made the mistake of being accompanied into her apartment by an almost unknown man - which means that he had put his foot in the door when she wanted to say goodbye. When he got pushy, she used all her intellectual knowledge to get him to leave, but it didn't help. Even quotations from the philosopher L. Wittgenstein ebbed away without reaction. Then she called for help or took her to a knife and apparently threatened very martially, and so the brutal type started the retreat. She was left with a "wild, raw, dangerous feeling of happiness," as she writes. Throughout her life, this scene clarified her basic statement: normal woman, ruthless man.

The question of why she locked up her apartment and didn't reject the semi-rapist downstairs in front of the house entrance is wrong. There must be a certain zone of commitment, even the modern 'no is no' has barely penetrated most men. The sexual pressure among young men is enormous, and no sex before marriage exists only in strict Muslim communities. Also my text here will not be able to say what a woman really is and how she can best come to herself. I can only refer again to the self-practical methodology, in which 'What about the ONE' makes possible the identity that applies to each individual and in different forms also to all.

Even Lacan's wonderful and strange formula about what a woman is cannot help here. For him, the formula $\forall x \Phi x$ means "the woman's demand that the man belongs entirely to her, because it is a woman's nature to be jealous".[79] Really? This is reminiscent of the Nobel Prize winner Proudhomme, Nobel Prize winner for literature, who said that "love is not worth serving as the theme of a great work; because it presupposes the ignorant, vain and frivolous woman".[80] How terrible! For him women were by nature somehow so pure, quasi sterile and inert, and thus could not be spoiled as such. Love was everything and nothing at the same time. For him it could never be realized, he loved only his sister all his life. No way out, either. But what did love mean for Siri Hustvedt?

In no way any expertise designed by men. But you don't have to say it as mathematically and crazy as with the formula $\forall x \Phi x$. In an interview with the ZEIT, Siri Hustvedt herself agrees that women must love men the way they loved their fathers.[81] But then she doesn't say what it was like with her father, whose death turned her into a 'trembling woman'. "The father is often only the

---

[79]The $\forall x \Phi x$ and additionally $\exists x \Phi x$ is a spelling of the quantor logic, an example of Lacan's approach. This is copied by the so-called Lacanians because they can't think of anything of their own. Everyone, men and women (Allquantor $\forall$) are subject to the same sexualization, but there could be one who is exempt from it (Exis-tenzquantor $\exists$), a primordial father, the general one, the universal Other. Only this enables the woman to be herself, so the result of Lacan's cumbersome and curious way of expression.

[80]Proudhomme, S., Intimes Tagebuch, Coron Verlag S. 60, 74

[81]Mayer, S., Siri Hustvedt, „Warum lieben sich Menschen? Ich habe keine Ahnung" (Why do people love each other? I have no idea"), ZEIT online vom 17. 3. 2011

third in the game," she says, and continues: "But it's always about that look of the other in which I recognize myself. We become ourselves through the glances of others". It sounds like a not quite correctly understood Lacan.

Because the important look here and now in this context is that of the body's own mirroring and not of the self in the other mirroring. It is about the gaze, which contains a completely body-hugging unconscious grasp of the image-real, the COO, while the father (the bodily, social) mediates the usual other, who can only give such a confirming, appreciative gaze towards a woman when his masculinity is elided. There is more to it than the conventional repression, because one does not or only very limitedly become oneself by the looks of the others as Siri Hustvedt says. One has really become oneself through the gaze of the COO, whom - if he is really captured - Lacan calls the "ultrasubjective radiance", the perfect It *Rays*. Or even more: the R*ays / Speaks*, the combination of the two sides of the *father-name* so often quoted by Lacan.

On the one hand, it is the look that pushed Moses to the ground when he blinded him in the 'burning thorn bush' on Sinai. Yet Moses could have perceived it in himself if he hadn't totally discarded this 'imaginary object', the COO. The rejection or the - in Freudian jargon so called - original repression is more elementary than the usual repression or denial. Therefore, from the very beginning and beyond the early years, few people have this 'archetypal object' at their disposal, which perhaps also contributed to Jeanne D'Arc, if they would not have had to cover it so clearly by a rigid male dominating and confessionally restricted education. After all, it was still visible with her. On the other hand, it's also about the name on the other hand, it's also about the name (that of the father, of the significant Other) that this *Rays*-Object gives of itself, that it *Speaks*.

I had some lesbian women in analytical psychotherapy and was amazed at how much the father was glorified, as if there had never been anything penetrantly-penetrating about him. They all had a high claim to love, i.e. I had the feeling that one should have confirmed to them again and again how positive, great, beautiful, wonderful etc. they were. But they suggested it through their stories, in which they already succeeded as children in Indian games through their strength and later - as Siri Hustveldt also notices - raved about the great thinkers. But isn't the father turned into a wonderful statue, a memorial, a heroic, but immobile and asexual statue?

For Siri Hustvedt, neurologists, psychiatrists and philosophers are such heroic figures who can be used like weapons, if necessary. In the above-mentioned interview in ZEIT-online she therefore also said: "There is great resistance among men to reading a book written by a woman. Once I said to such a man, "Could we have a look at what you said for a moment? You don't read Homer, Dante, Shakespeare - I made a really long list out of it - is it something you just don't like? Do you think it's silly? Stupid"?

ZEIT: What was his answer?

"There were none. He fell silent! Because if you take out the big gun, these guys will of course back down," Siri Hustvedt skillfully replied in her classic, feminist manner. There's nothing to say against that, she obviously usually meets such men, but of course men are basically the wrong people to talk to. She would have needed a good cultural philosopher, anthropologist or psychoanalyst who, if necessary - as Judith Le Soldat has shown - would get the most hidden incest or hidden cannibalism out of the unconscious. On the one hand. Because on the other hand I understand well and have already said it in such a way that one cannot bring the psychological trauma into the daylight in a way, where it becomes traumatizing again. And when Siri Hustvedt writes about suffering from the soul, it is probably sufficient.

I have already reported on multiple orgasms. "It is extremely important," Siri Hustvedt finally says in the ZEIT interview on this subject, "that women also become aware of their own sexism. . . . There are neurologists, among them only a few women, who sit together and deny all females in the animal kingdom their own orgasm. Unbelievable"! And further in the FAZ of 8. 11. 2018: "It is strange how male superiority is formulated. Women, for example, are very potent when it comes to their ability to orgasm, but the fact that women can be very persistent in bed and achieve great satisfaction is not regarded as power".

"Women these days live longer than men. That is not considered superior either. All differences are interpreted to the advantage of men. And so one prefers to describe the female orgasm as complicated? But it is not complicated at all. Although I recently read that some young men are also capable of multiple orgasms. For women, this ability is interpreted as complicated so that you don't even have to deal with the idea of such an overwhelming superpower. And because men are always the aggressive, active part in our eyes, women must not take the first step? Even for my daughter's generation this is still true. Sex must be initiated by the man. Why then"?[82]

Poor Siri Hustvedt, there must be a misunderstanding, as there is no gender relationship at all. Of course bad things happen there, but is orgasm not the wrong expression for a woman, when it's about the 'jouissance', which is close to 'What about the ONE'. What usually means orgasm, this unfortunate 'plaisir phallique', doesn't mean that the woman has to take on this 'power', this activism, only to be able to say that she also has it. Why power? Sexual pride, potency, a certain power is involved, which is already infantile enough. The men have the orgasm and the women enjoy it - as the Hite report showed: they enjoy landscapes, colours, levitations, beautiful eyes, flights of fancy, full-body trickling and much more. Helene Deutsch, a student of Freud, was already amused by the fact that one had to stimulate the female genitals in order to awaken the pleasure.

During sex, women also occasionally think in peace about what to buy and whom to call. Why shouldn't they

---

[82]Kray, Sabine, Interview mit Siri Hustvedt. ‚Man muss sich schon mal die Hände schmutzig machen' (You have to get your hands dirty'), FAZ vom 8. 11. 2018

be allowed to do that? In numerous studies[83] - mostly via questionnaires - the women confirmed that emotional satisfaction is more important to them than orgasm. I quote here only a work - and admittedly - last truths cannot be found here, and are mostly too superficial. In her latest book, Siri Hustvedt once says that sexual pleasure is a huge thing and bursts into laughter because she doesn't quite believe it herself. None of this is complicated, it's just a deception, a shine like the mating dances of the animals, which are nothing more than a great and often enduring spectacle for the following extremely short process of pairing. Just like death at sacrifice, ugliness at mating puts us in fear,"[84] the queerly philosopher G. Bataille stated in relation to man.

In the book just quoted, Siri Hustvedt comments on many of her thoughts, including that of her neurosis, which she herself calls hysteria.[85] In long passages she explains which symptoms are typical for her and others, how psychoanalysis has helped her to become freer and how suffering is still a mystery. She also tells in detail that she is still researching how the conversion typical of hysteria occurs in the brain, forcing the concept of a 'body-subject' that is a social, psychological and biological entity and discussing more material and more spiritual approaches

---

[83]Langer, D., Langer S., Sexuell gestörte und sexuell zufriedene Frauen (Sexually disturbed and sexually satisfied women), Verlag Hans Huber Bern (1988) S. 22

[84]Bataille, G., Die Erotik, Matthes Seitz (1994) S. 140f

[85]Hustvedt, S., Wenn Gefühle auf Worte treffen (When feelings meet words) Kampa (2019) S. 79

to the problem of neuroses. In so doing, she completely forgets to access her own good and suitable metaphors and concepts, namely that of 'in-between-ness'. Because there, only there, the hysteria arises, which in my opinion, supported by Lacan, is nothing else than an early identification with the opposite sex!

It's as simple as that, even if the same things happen in the brain and in the social sphere, but these are side scenes. Everybody knows that a woman who has a certain style - it doesn't have to be theatrical - rather a brash, somehow not quite believable appearance, something slightly boastful with sexual freedom, but who basically doesn't want to be used at all, shows that the male sex is copied here. But as raw as it actually is, it is not brought into female existence at all. This castling, exchange action, often reminiscent of a transsexual, looks as if the woman were the virile partner of a lesbian, but in reality she wants to impress the man, wants to persuade him to a firm relationship.

The hysterical man is no different. He wants to be gallant, soft, flexible, playful and witty, but the actor is the feminine-hysterical melodramatist who attracts everyone's attention. He looks like the queer gay, although he seems to have nothing in mind with homosexuality.[86] The women are supposed to fall in love with the softie, the charming man, who often has a problem with his potency, and so she feels like Elsa von Brabant with Lohengrin in R. Wagners opera, who was also such a smart guy. "Lohengrin, as you know, forbids asking who

---

[86]Which is often the shadow of his neurosis.

he is. And typically on the wedding night he can no longer avoid the answer: that he is impotent, that he fails. The whole thing starts with the fact that Elsa von Brabant only wants a man whom God has chosen! That's schizophrenic! Of course she had to ask him on the wedding night, 'What's the matter with you?' He collapsed and blamed his sexual failure on the woman."[87]

Siri Hustvedt is right when she equates this 'in-between-ness' with Freudian transference, because the oscillation of transference/countertransference also between child and parents creates such neuroses quite well, even if the parents have completely different mental structures that appear more adapted. Behind the facades the same game is raging everywhere, which also happens in the social sphere and is also promoted by the biological. But the main characteristic of hysteria is the early identification with the opposite sex, with the sexual other. Not much will change the fact that Siri Hustvedt "always felt both as well as, female and male. I am neither one nor the other. I hate to be put in a drawer, no matter which one".[88]

But will that work? After all, she puts herself in the drawer of the hysterical woman, who suffers precisely from this complex of masculinity, which Freud, in the sense of his drive-structure concept, stated to be one of women's life paths. The other two were frigidity and

---

[87]Quoted after a passage in my book 'Die Mathematik des Eros', BoD (2018)
[88]Hustvedt, S., Wenn Gefühle auf Worte treffen (When feelings meet words) Kampa (2019) S. 79

motherhood. Sounds terrible these days, of course.[89] But isn't it a bit awkward when Siri Hustvedt, in addition to her great way of being a woman, also wants so much masculinity that she has the same amount of both. She doesn't want to be the woman who represents all of them, because she knows too well that this isn't possible and would be all too curious. But let her be more postgender, she mainly wants to be a great author and also a scientist and appears successfull in these functions in readings all over the world. And why shouldn't she continue to do that better? There's not much room for androgyny anyhow. So she succeeds quite well as wife and author, with being a scientist there is still a bit of a problem. On the one hand, she says that humans are 'thinking bodies', which is exactly the Cartesian view she rejected, in which Descartes said, 'I am a thinking thing'.

No, no, she will say, I mean it differently, namely that mind and body are not completely separate. But then how are they connected? Siri Hustvedt quotes V. Woolf, who would adhere to the Panpsychism and in whom "matter thinks, but not machine-like. Simply brilliant! Is that enough? Spaces in dreams she describes as such as in reality, because these and the memories must always take place somewhere local. But doesn't Einstein's geometry prevail in the dream, prevail as topology, where the

---

[89]That doesn't exclude the possibility that the woman is also a wonderful wife, an outstanding pianist, teacher and God knows what else can be. Freud is only concerned with certain unconscious identities acquired in early childhood, which he perceives too socially conditioned, since he did not know these earliest reflections.

spatial is knotted, rolled up and nested in itself? It cannot be fixed locally, so that completely different perspectives emerge, e.g. those where something speaks? This is then important for the dream reader. And so Siri Hustvedt comes to her currently most exciting field of research, the placenta.

She believes that umbilical cord and placenta are not only a biological 'in-between-ness' of mother and child, but much, much more. Umbilical cord and placenta are first and foremost only childlike tissue. The child has anchored itself with its placenta villi in the tissue of the uterus. At birth, the child loses less the mother than a large part of its own body, which is the placenta. One would have to start psychoanalytically, from the 'lost object', and would have to talk about the first serious splitting and fear of loss, which sounds very much like the own body mirrorings, which here would have a correlate in the real body. Only, mirrorings can be processed. Do you really want to have the placenta back?

I could perhaps recommend to Siri Hustvedt the field of research into the nature of Transgender. I think you can get more out of it than from researching the placenta. As far as transgender, the transsexual, is concerned, this does not really fit into the Freudian scheme. Freud had spoken in his books more than once about the "phallic phase" in the development of the child, which meant that in both sexes this form of psycho-sexual development, ascribed somewhat more to the male, takes place, even if this has different interpretations. Transgender thus lies beyond the phallic, which is the same for man and woman and is therefore also suitable for counting, i.e. for the mathematics of eros. In transgender, the phallic libido can no longer be regarded as the common currency.

With the modern discussion about transgender or trans-identity, the theory about the essence of the sexes has also become an important topic in psychoanalysis. This means that psychoanalysis in particular has a lot to say here, because what identity really means in relation to instincts or desires, what symbolic means in relation to real things, what fantasies, feelings as "psychic reality" in relation to material things as "physical reality" means, can only be determined from the very personal, private, subject-related conversations in such a science.

I have already mentioned the research of the psychoanalyst Judith Le Soldat and have pointed out that in her books she has established transgender-related theories, but still expressed them very mythically. At the beginning of life, the sphinx-like mother figure plunges the still immature childlike soul into unsolvable conflicts, because both protagonists (male-animal mother and child) allow the different organs to act simultaneously sexual-imaginary. Unconsciously a kind of castration lust comes about, the child wants to rob this sphinx-like being - to understand everything still unconsciously - of its perpetual pleasure, but with so much sadism of its own it threatens itself at the same time with fear of punishment and confusion.

In order to arrive at psychoanalytical interpretations at all, Le Soldat had to elicit corresponding fantasies from her patients, which seemed a bit manipulative. As already mentioned, I think that Le Soldat's psychoanalysis is probably only considered a therapy in special cases. This also seems to be the case in the recent transgender discussion. With A. Limentani, J. Kesten-berg, G. Hansbury and other psychoanalytical authors, attempts have been made to investigate the transgender topic under the aspect of self-body mirroring. If the men already have an envy for the libido which closes in the women in them to the circle, then the authors mentioned see with men, who have the desire to be a woman mostly a strong envy for all feminine, particularly also for the assumed 'feminine enjoyment', often equipped with the fantasy to have a vagina.

This attitude is often associated with a pronounced 'orality' (mouth, devouring-, merging lust). Hansbury, who works a lot with transgender persons and is himself a transman (i.e. was previously biologically a woman), postulated that all men - quite analogously to the findings of Judith Le Soldat - possess a so-called "masculine vaginal", i.e. a female kind of sexuality, which he also described quite oppositely as an "inner spiritual space".[90] Thus it is clearly delimited that it is not about the real organ, but about something imaginary/symbolic, an image and language space, as it can ideally be understood from the primary or self body mirroring.

This imaginary reality dominates Hansbury's work, everything is perforated and transformed by phantasmatic sexual body images, by invaginations and bulges of different gender types. The "queer men", says Hansbury,

[90]Hansbury, G., The masculine Vaginal, Journal American Psychoanalysis 65 (2018), p. 1009-1031

for example, "must first learn that it is not the vagina on which transmen, for example, remain in indifference. The crucial thing is that this "masculine vaginal", the inner sexual space of desire in which another man or woman can, so to speak, implant himself directly, is important for the ultimate, summary psycho-sexual identity that he calls "inclusion". This theory sounds rather abysmal and probably only applies to the sexual therapy of queer men.

But perhaps what applies to queer men could not also apply - with reversed signs - to erotomaniac women or women too strongly influenced by feminism, no matter whether they are cis or trans. For they presume this finished 'inclusion' to themselves, they believe in sexual omnipotence (the androgyne). The "masculine vaginal" must then be confronted as a counterpart on the female side with something like the "phallic woman", whose relationship to the more active "plaisier phallique" has been provided with the corresponding envy on the part of the woman. It is well known that Freud spoke quite misleadingly about the woman's "penis envy". In this respect, however, it is a male dynamic that forces the man to deal with his desire. For this dynamic one can perhaps envy him. He must sublimate the outwardly directed too much sexual activity, he must - as the philosopher M. Foucault said - transform the active into a "power without ruler (without rule) and the sexist into a sex without law (without standardization)".

All this - the female inner libidinal circle and the male dynamic - fit much better to the "inner spiritual space", in that it - if one still wants to remain on the transgendered level - also includes fertility, creativity, yes, as I already quoted from the psychoanalyst R. Golan, also suffering, universality, knowledge, freedom and bliss.[91] This space is more close to the real of the 'jouissance', for which one would no longer have to transgender. One must therefore say quite clearly that all these attributions only make sense if they take place in a practised therapy, in a 'logical practice', especially for persons with a pronounced transgender problem. For normal use as philosophical, cultural, generally psychological representation, they have significance only in their metaphor. For Lacan and for my *Analytic Psychocatharsis* borrowed from psychoanalysis, other terms make sense. The only good thing about Hansbury and the other authors is that they rely on the primary body reflection and the primary resounding, the 'sound' of the body echoes. And only this can be recommended to Siri Hustvedt.

So what I am writing here is the essence of my scientific experience, and there the "inner-mental space" is not necessarily occupied by the "female phallic" or "masculine vaginal". For me it is the place of the above-mentioned fertility, the creativity, universality and that of a sovereign love, a love that does not have to reveal itself, a 'detached love'. This love bridges the splitting from which I basically proceed, in that the subject, the human being related to his or her subjectivity, is precisely transferred into the loosely separated body mirrorings and reflections of the self, into the imaginary, but must also be at home in the symbolic. Freud-Lacan's driving

---

[91]Golan, R. Loving Psychoanalysis, Karnak (2006)

concept already assumes two basic driving forces in humans. One spoke of the perceptual or viewing instinct on the one hand and the expelling or speaking instinct on the other. Such an elementary dualism is used everywhere in science and even generally in the form of the humanities and natural sciences.

I would also like to add that A. Ferrari, whom I have already quoted several times by his COO, regards the self-in-alteration reflection as the "horizontal relation", because it is reflected in the outside of social, emotional, business relations, while the 'concrete object of origin' (COO) of the primary body-own mirroring is referred to by him as the "vertical relation". We are used to the outwardly directed horizontal ego, we have split off the vertical self, forgotten it, although it would be so important. I have therefore dedicated an own book to the vertical ego.

Already the philosopher P. Sloterdijk has dealt with this personality structure, he uses only the terms somewhat differently, than I described it so far. So he makes fun when it comes to the body image, the body scheme, which he calls the so-called 'vertical tension' and which probably has to do with the 'vertical relationship scheme' of which A. Ferrari speaks.[92] The 'above', the 'higher' and 'over' - not only that of body feelings, but also that of religions and philosophies, probably also that of his own - inspire him to make mocking remarks. Jakob's sky ladder but also the 'depth psychology' are situated in a vertical for which, according to Sloterdijk's view, there is

---

[92]Sloterdijk, P., Du musst dein Leben ändern, Suhrkamp (2009)

actually no clear justification. All attempts to give form to this vertical tension always end only in acrobatics, in constantly new exercise methods and 'anthropotechnic techniques', which are based on a puzzling 'summit urge', he writes.

Sloterdijk calls the 'vertical tension' the 'intellectual correspondence' of the horizontal, but that is a typically philosophical view. He cannot imagine ego formation as such an important body mirroring as it is described by many authors in the meantime, but sees it only in highly screwed up thoughts. Obviously, however, Sloterdijk's concept of the tension of the vertical is based precisely on this 'concrete object of origin', but he knows nothing about it. He lacks the medical and above all the psychoanalytical background. The philosopher himself writes in another book about the 'distancing self-inclusion' or the 'self-isolation effect' of the hominid groups in the world,[93] which clearly points to the primary self-body mirroring. But the philosopher does not understand their importance, because he has recognized them among the early men and the hominids, whom he considers to be inferior.

Because the hominids, but also the early humans, had to withdraw into themselves, they first became humans, he says as a supplement to his thesis of ',foaming of the brain", which I mentioned at the beginning. Self-enclosure, withdrawal, however, means especially those in the body schematic vertical, because where else should

---

[93]Sloterdijk, P., Sphären III, Suhrkamp (2004) S. 359

one be able to self-enclose and withdraw? It would now be easy to point out yoga, Zen Buddhism and all the procedures where the vertical is also so emphasized. This is precisely the function of the sushumna in yoga, in which the 'main energy flow' moves vertically in the middle (see the figure below, where I also made a comparison with psychoanalysis).

Siri Hustvedt could be explained that the masculinity she is certainly entitled to is not something phallic that she has, rather she personifies it herself from a male point of view anyway, and for this one basically does not need a specific masculinity in addition. One must - if one wants to remain with Freud's phallic - rather start from the primary view into the inner mental space, which can also echo from male sounds and phrases. For the feminists often deny, as I said, that the phallic is a signifier, a symbolic object, that is, the symbolic part of the inner-soul space that also speaks. This also contains a certain 'queer-ness', one between the ray and the speech, Siri Hustvedt's "in-between-ness", i.e. another than that used in the transgender

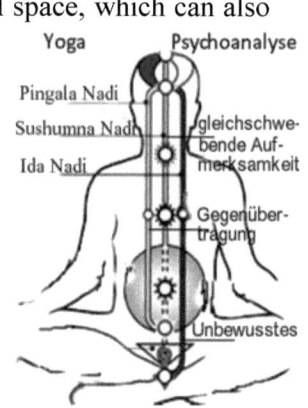

discussion but also in the general man/woman difference. But this "in-between-ness" is vertical!

Nevertheless, this discussion could perhaps also inspire Siri Hustvedt's research, because neuroscientific and psychiatric sciences will only be able to contribute insufficiently to the male/female problem. Above all, it would be much better not to always examine the brain neuroscientifically, but to fathom the structure of the soul in the direction in which it can transform the plasticity of the brain. The philosopher A. Noë writes in his book "You are not your brain" that today we are much too impressed by the neurosciences. We are neuro-film and synapses-hearing. For A. Noë, consciousness and the soul are primarily not in the individual, in the brain standing alone, but in the connex and context in which the brain stands and dynamically interacts with its environment and other brains.

This connection/context therefore occurs rather in a kind of typographic space or hyperspherical grammar, precisely this mental interior of the reflections and echoes, to which the brains probably have a somewhat more intensive and complex relationship than another cell network. With this, I want to recognize once again the justification of the neurosciences; they are only too little related to the real, contextual subject. They are not a science from the subject. They do not show the great therapeutic possibilities. The inner mental space is typographical / hyperspherical and not occupied by transgenders. Man and woman are not only genetic, but are also therefore preordained.

T. Schachl has formulated it even more ideally when she describes the movement, which runs "in different stages of visibility: from the diagnosis transsexual via the pre-operative transsocial phase of outing and arriving in the quasi invisible completely normal".[94] Although Schachl is a "metaphor researcher", expert on phonemes and their reverberation, she recognizes that the transgender problem lies in "the emphasis on 'seeing', 'visibility' and 'images'", in short: in the self-reflection in the Other outside. She speaks of the 'banner of visibility', "for which a tremendously high price is paid", in order to be able to present this perfect image of what is revolving around the two corners of the sexual and the most normal possible. For in reality transgender people, like all others, end up in an 'invisibility' that remains silent around the two corners, writes Schachl. The transgender doesn't feel perceived in his first sex, doesn't feel confirmed, and so for this confirmation and for the sake of truth, he now tries to change sex, because he has seen and believes that it will function in this form, will function normally. The emphasis is on being seen and standardization.

When I read Siri Hustvedt's books I sometimes get the temptation to have to 'queer' her good literature, which would be terrible. But maybe it would help her to see it that way. Usually we only talk about man/woman and masculinity/femininity, with which Siri Hustvedt struggles endlessly. At best, it is still stated that the masculine is more coordinated with the wordlike, the language-processing, the feminine more with the pictorial, the image-processing. But how do two brains

---

[94]Schachl, T., Transsexuell, eine sichtbare Bewegung ins Un-sichtbare (Transsexual, a Visible Movement into the Invisible), Profil (1997)

coordinate, typographically, topologically, comparatistically? What does the relevant connection/context look like, which mystics always wanted to see in the fact that one must have "the heart in the forehead", i.e. further up, but still intimately. According to Freud, this should also be so, "where It was I should become (in the spirit)".

In order to clarify and optimize this coordination scientifically and not only mystically, all the different areas will be coordinated in life, and the final combination will then be achieved rather than with the functions and symbols of the placenta or the transgender sexual with something like the formula and passport words of *Analytic Psychocatharsis*. Here is an example from my own experience. While practicing with these formula words, after listening to myself for a while (to a tone, to a statement, to the speech), which is the second exercise, I once caught the following ultra-reduced phrase: " You shall be Adam". This won't mean much to any outsider, but I immediately realized what was meant. As a doctor and psychoanalyst, I didn't make a career. Neither in the natural sciences nor in the mental sciences (if I may now count psychoanalysis as one of them) could I somehow be particularly successful.

But apparently I had the ambition to become someone who should have a say in the scientific discussion of the time or who didn't just want to work as a backbencher. The thing with Adam was clear to me and just right with regard to this still missing identity. After all, Lacan demasked all the "university discourses" as outdated and, because he was passing by the actual truth, only as purely knowledge-addicted. But to be an Adam meant to start again where mankind began with knowledge and wisdom. It meant to be the first human being again, by starting from the biblical mythology as the spiritual-scientific as well as from the paleoanthropology as the natural-scientific in the sense of a new beginning, in order to establish a practical anthropology.

The philosopher N. Knapp describes very wittily how the grandmother wanted to read to her as a child something of the first humans.[95] Since she had already read some of the Neanderthals and the early humans herself, she was looking forward to further stories from paleoan-thropology. But to her horror, the grandmother began with the story of Adam and Eve. Only later did it become clear to her that both approaches to the beginning of mankind are equally valuable and that one has to fathom one's own superior approach.

For this you have to include your own unconscious, which makes this 'transubstantiation' possible. For me, there was also a conscious intention behind being Adam, but I would never have expressed it that way in general com-munication. I would have said, and sometimes I have already thought it, that one would have to be able to start all over again with a primordial culture like the first humans. But the early humans certainly did not yet possess a culture or religion in the conventional sense. Their ideas of superordinate powers were based on animistic experiences and probably not on concrete

---

[95]Knapp, N., Der Quantensprung des Denkens (The Quantum Leap of Thought), Rowohlt (2011)

figures of gods. The gods and above all the monotheistic God have made life different, but not easier,

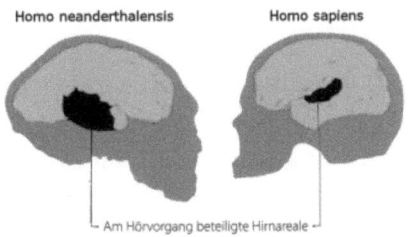

Homo neanderthalensis   Homo sapiens

— Am Hörvorgang beteiligte Hirnareale —

After all, the earliest beings who could be given the name Homo knew burial rituals and other social operationalizations. Not for nothing did I spend much time on the Neanderthal. He was already human in the full sense of the word, since he possessed language to a sufficient degree and thus also had an unconscious mind. He was incredibly robust and close to nature and also had a bigger brain than we did. He used it only so laboriously and very much brain mass in the Temporo-Ocipital area used (sensorimotor system), in order to make itself understandable, in addition, in order to be able to experience the things very intensively.[96] I think he was Adam, too, because he understood nature as a unified being, as something 'what about the ONE'.

The direct comparison of the figure above shows that the brain area responsible for processing electrical impulses

---

[96]Czarnetzki, A., Der Neandertaler – eine hochspezialisierte Art (The Neanderthal - a highly specialized species). www.ar-chaeologieonline.de/magazin/thema/2001/06/c_1.

from the inner ear was more space-filling than that of modern Homo sapiens. As mentioned above, the Neanderthal is said to have been able to hear "the sound of the wind in the needles", whether it was a fir or a pine. So he actually had something of the 'speaks' of absolute hearing in him.[97] He still perceived with the music of the forest, with the echo of the "sound object" as such. And it should have been the same with his visual abilities. Czarnitzki writes that the Neanderthal was "excellently trained for the perception of optical impressions such as optic thing recognition, sense of place, local memory, recognition of colour and brightness, etc., but also for optic thoughts. Classic case of the use of COO, the self-body reflection.

But as far as my password is concerned, it would not have been so intense, so revealing for me to have the intention to be like an early man again in the context of these thoughts and researches. For that would have meant entering into a quasi phylogenetic regression and reformulating human history from there. Also I had no desire from the religion of the Old Testament, which I rather call denominations, to win an identity for today and to try a new beginning.

I would have had to have something of a revelation. And even if I could say that this "ultra-reduced phrase" of "Shall be the Adam" sounds almost like an off-screen saying, I would not only have remained untrustworthy to others, but also to myself. I see the classical revelations

[97]Czarnetzki, A., Oral Announcement and Surrender of the above Figure) 11.05.09

as a collection of pass words from the unconscious of these prophets and founders of religions against the background and as a consequence of deep ancestor worship. But we no longer have this very approach today, and the Off as a modern variant of this view is also no longer very plausible.

Nevertheless, the unconscious was the same then as it is today. It is a "linguistic crystal" of contrapuntal thoughts (Freud speaks of anticathexis). To be Adam - taken simply and only in reference to his sound of words from the unconscious - was all that I had just discussed opposite, a much more gaudy, intense thought, indeed an originally real name, a much more vivid identity. Being Adam was a password, a proper name in the sense of 'What about the ONE', because Adam was and is more than just a mythical figure.

Adam was himself one of those early men, homo sapiens, perhaps even before the Cro-Magnon types we are today, but with a special endowment. He must have achieved an overview of the living beings on this earth and at the same time felt this to be something like a "mission", an invitation to be human. And as such an invitation I also perceived it. "You shall be an early man" would have frightened me, and I would not have wanted to be a successor of Abraham, Isaac and Jacob either, but Adam as such, as ONE,[98] fit for both, for an early and a modern identity of comprehensive kind.

---

[98]This means only the One that is valid for me in this pass-word name

So Adam is doing a much better job here. For me here ideal mediator for the first human being, neurotic, not yet finished, driven out of the paradise of childhood and belief in a certain positive politics or other science, but like the Neanderthal, already provided with an unconscious (subordinated to the symbolic order) and highly sensitive. My unconscious has here originally and for me surprisingly well brought the radiance / speech into something 'transsubstantiating' and I can therefore recommend the exercises of *Analytic Psychocatharsis* to everyone.

Maybe it could also help Siri Hustvedt, because she, who says that she suffers from a 'mirror-touch-synesthesia', would quickly be successful with it. In the first exercise, where one exposes oneself to the nothing, the zero, and approaches 'what there is of the ON' in catharsis, she would already have a strong touching experience, because no touch (as Roazens 'inner touch') is as intense as that of the nothing, the dark before one in meditation, or 'what there is of the ON', even if it is not quite there yet. People with a high degree of empathy always react stronger, more direct in the first exercise. I would remind you that the repetition of the formula words, which give security through their scientific justification, do not allow for a negative experience.

I think that the example of my password and my thoughts on it show why I rightly speak here of the fact that one can find with it 'What about the ONE', and that it is only from this subject position, only from this subject-related science, possible to continue to work with the ultimate identity. It is not enough just to explore the mind, to paint it fantastically, to clarify it psychoanalytically, to process it neuroscientifically, literarily or philosophically; one must also make it happy.

Appendix

The procedure of *Analytic Psychocatharsis* is very simple from its practical side - as already described in part. Nevertheless, I will give here a short summary and further formula words.[99] You sit in a comfortable posture and repeat one, two or up to five formula words slowly one after the other purely in your mind, while at the same time you pay attention to whether something appears that has the character of an 'It *Rays*'. The "ray" can be an enlightenment, body image perception, a shimmer, a 'spot of light', or a basic lucidity that is associated with such a phenomenon. So the ray is not something you have to imagine, create or even force yourself. It is present in every human being as the primary form of a force event (drive) and thus only has to be awakened or expected. In the same way, a 'trickling through' can also be felt or the sensation can emerge how one's own body image shifts,[100] widens or is simply fixed as black paint, as a stain in front of the closed eyes. Because black is already

---

[99]Further formula words can be found in other publications or on the website given below. For the time being, these are sufficient. You should not need more than five.

[100]This is an experience that has something to do with atavistic emotional reactions. The early humans still felt a lot with their uncovered skin, touched it and communicated in an environment-related way. Even with moving pieces of music, when it grips you like a shiver trickling down your back, we fall back on these particularly deep emotions. In *Analytic Psychocatharsis*, however, this experience is used as confirmation of an insight, e.g. in the pass-words.

a perception, which can stand out from the darkness in the head quite slightly. No matter what is 'seen' or 'experienced', it will have the character of even a very small 'it *Rays*', and that is enough.

Thus a relaxation occurs, a catharsis, a liberation experience, which can be increased especially if at the same time the said formula words are practiced purely mentally. At the bottom left you can see another formula word. Also this (RA-DIC-IT) is not a normal word from Latin, but it contains several overlapping meanings in one formulation, it is 'linguistically crystalline' like Lacan said from the unconscious. Besides the radiat and dicit (radiates and speaks) there are several disparate meanings written in a circle and read from different letters. For example, here one can also use "adi cit r" (approach, it moves R), "C i tradi" (handed over a hundred I), "citra di" (on this side the gods), "dicit ra" (it says ra), "r adic it" (add r, it goes), "radi cit" (get scratched, it moves), "trad ici" (tell, I have met) etc., whereby much sounds quite absurd. But this has no meaning for the formal expression. It is only decisive to be able to clearly explain the scientific reasoning (several meanings in one formulation, use only of other interfaces), and this is very important for the procedure, because this is the only way to have full confidence in the method.

This is the first exercise which is based on actual guidelines of psychoanalysis, because mental reverberation generates a regression (an inner retreat) which at the same time concentrates only on a narrowed aspect of the perceptual instinct (the *Rays*). In addition, formula-word repetition takes the place of what in psychoanalysis is called the obligation to repeat, the unconscious repetition. This is at least abolished as long as the exercises of the *Analytic Psychocatharsis* are effective. I have already indicated in the main text that this simplifies and reduces an essential hurdle of classical psychoanalysis. It is important that it comes to a catharsis, to a liberation experience and not only to a simple relaxation. At least for some time one frees oneself from the unconscious obligation to repeat.

As far as other forms of therapy and their problems are concerned, by using *Analytic Psychocatharsis* it is usually possible to avoid them in a simplified way. It is no longer enough simply to believe a therapist or meditation teacher and follow his simple instructions. Nowadays it is also necessary to understand that the method has a scientific basis and that one can and should participate with own thoughts. This way, in deeper moments of the exercises dependencies on the ideology of the method, on the teacher or therapist or irrational fears do not occur. The *Rays* (crystalline) of the cathartic experience are thus derived from the basic power of the scopic drive. [101] It is therefore something that is originally

---

[101] In psychoanalysis we assume that symbolic order or language plays a decisive role in human development, dividing perception into a pure sensory activity and a drive activity. The activity of the senses is a real perception, the activity of instinct a pleasure of perception, in summary we speak of perceptiveness. The true comes in through language (It *Speaks*), the perception through reality (It radiates).

present in every human being, just like the *Speaks* (the linguistic, the uttering).

After the R-A-D-I-C-I-T, the formula word O-R-S-A-C-E-R-A-M can be added, because if someone is really interested in learning the analytic pychocathartic method, at least three of these formulations are necessary. Two or even just one would tire you out too quickly. In the formula-word C-E-R-A-M-O-R-S-A (picture previous page) - once written differently - there are following meanings depending on initial letter: C eram orsa (I was a hundred times beginning, amo R sacer (I love the holy R), cera morsa (the fragmented wax), mors acer (death is bitter), amor sacer (love is holy), etc.). How to

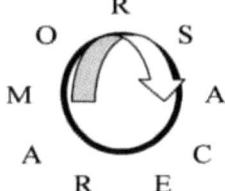

emphasize, one can forget these meanings immediately again. They are too disparate, i.e. cannot be reduced to any denominator. For if one practices them in the uniform lettering, one will never bring together the 'bitter death' with the 'fragmented wax' and the 'hun-dredfold beginning' in only one meaning. It is only important to understand how the formula words are structured, so that one can scientifically-intellectually question the process of any time. If any feelings or ideas arise that are inappropriate or frightening, one can reflect or read more about the process. Blind faith is not required.

In the second exercise, attention is now paid to exactly this speech, this body echo, i.e. to a sound coming from above / right in the head, to a tone, sound, from the deep inside. After all, these are letters that emanate from this 'typographic' space and which the unconscious holds stored there. And it is precisely into this space that the formula words have penetrated and have awakened and evoked the letters in their B(r)uchstaben-likeness (broken-letterings). Again, the same applies here: it is a completely original aspect of the drive to express or speak, which is present in every human being as a primary process and even takes on the form of very brief, compact "inner sentences", "ultra-reduced phrases" in the unconscious (all concepts of Lacan for this phonetic experience).

Here, too, at first only a fine noise, a distant sound or similar can be perceived, but the practitioner will notice from the beginning that this is a concentration on a more up-right or up-central hearing system in the head. The echoes of the body have a relationship to this, which is being referred to here. Even if the actual hearing and speech system in the head is left-handed, the more rudimentary, musical and more regression accessible hearing and speech system is present on the right side and its echo structure is clearly recognizable. The short phrases of the pass-words are more suitable for this, while the left-sided system (psychoanalytically: the preconscious) plays a role in the longer ones.

If you read something about psychoanalysis and keep in touch with literary, scientific and other cultures, and have also read the present text, made an attempt with the exercises, in short: if you are a bit of an educated citizen, you will interpret the often immediately visible passwords correctly. Thus Freud writes that even some dreams, which are now much more distorted than the passwords, and which come directly from the symbolic-real, could be read directly from the "sheet". It is no longer necessary to ask the dreamer about his ideas and to bring in cumbersome interpretations.

And one last hint, which is often asked for. If one notices during the application of *Analytic Psychocatharsis* that the it *Rays* portion during practice is too strong, one switches to the it *Speaks* exercise and vice versa. Otherwise, both exercises should only be performed for about twenty minutes. The change between practical experience and theoretical thinking is important because in the end something in common will emerge: a mental self-awareness, a practical logic, a cathartic analysis. In the end, both exercises find their way to an inner 'mission', to a certainty of 'What about the ONE', and thus to the possibility of being able to participate in the procedure.

On the other hand, I have already described that sometimes one does not only deviate from the meditative process in thoughts. Sometimes one even deviates between the individual formula words to images, memories, to a mixture of both and to pass words, and yet returns to formula word reversion. The advanced student will experience this as enriching, because he does not allow himself to be seduced into a one-sided direction of radiation or speech, but remains in the progression in the narrow combination of the two basic drives, basic principles, mirroring- and echo-discourse.

On my website you can find numerous articles and hints about *Analytic Psychocatharsis*, partly also in English language.

Website: analytic-psychocatharsis.com

Bibliography

Baggini, J., Ich denke, also will ich, (I think, so I want) dtv (2016)

Barkhaus, A., Mayer, M., Identität, Leiblichkeit, Normativität (identity, corporeality, normativity(Suhrkamp (1996)

Bauriedl, T., Beziehungsanalyse, (relationship analysis) Suhrkamp (1993)

Benthien, C., Wulf, Ch., Körperteile (body parts), Rowohlt (2001)

Bezzel, C., Wittgenstein, Junius (1996)

Breuer, R., Immer Ärger mit dem Urknall (Always Trouble with the Big Bang), Rowohlt (1993)

Brockman, J., Vogel, S., Wie funktioniert die Welt? (How does the world work), Fi-scher Taschenbuch (2013)

Byung-Chul Han, Die Austreibung des Anderen (The Expulsion of the Other), Fischer Wissenschaft (201)

Byung-Chul Han, Die Errettung des Schönen (The Salvation of Beauty), Fischer Wissenschaft (201)

Camus, A., Der Mythos des Sisyphos, Rowohlt (2018)

Carnap, R., Einführung in die Philosophie der Naturwissenschaft (Introduction to the Philosophy of Natural Science) (1969)

Damasio, A. R., Descartes` Irrtum, Dtv (1997)

Dennet, D. C., Von den Bakterien zu Bach – und zurück, Suhrkamp (2018)

Davies, P., Gott und die moderne Physik (God and modern physics), Bert. M. (1986)

Eccles, J. C., Gehirn und Seele, Piper (1987)

Eichmeier, J., Höfer, O., Endogene Bildmuster, U&S – Verlag (1974)

Fischer-Lichte, E., Performativität: Eine Einführung, transcript (2012)

Freud, S., Studienausgabe, Fischer (1989)

Goel, B. S. Meditation und Psychoanalyse, Ariston (1989)

Görz, G., Einführung in die Künstliche Intelligenz (Introduction to Artificial Intelligence), Addison-Wesley (1996)

Harari, Y. N., Homo Deus, C. H. Beck (2017)

Heidegger, M., Unterwegs zur Sprache, G. Neske (1959)

Hilbrecht, H., Meditation und Gehirn, Schattauer (2010)

Hofstadter, D., Die Analogie, Klett-Cotta (2014)

Horgan, J., An den Grenzen des Wissens, Luchterhand (1997)

Hustvedt, S., Die gleissende Welt (The blazing Wiorld) Rowohlt (2016)

Husttvedt, S., Das Leiden eines Amerikanmers, Rowohlt (2009)

Hustvedt, S., Wenn Gefühle auf Worte treffen (When feelings meet words) , Kampa (2019)

Jacobs, A., Schrott, R., Gehirn und Gedicht, Hanser (2011

Jakobson, R., Semiotik, Suhrkamp (1988)

Jakobson, R., On Language, Harvard University Press (1995)

Jung. C.G., Gesammelte Werke, Walter (1983)

Kant, I., Kritik der reinen Vernunft, Reclam (1966)

Kluge, F., Etymologisches Wörterbuch, W. de Gruyter (1989)

Lacan, J., Schriften I - III, Walter, (1975)

Lacan, J., Seminare I,I, VII, XI, XX, Quadriga (1980-1995)

Lacan, J., Seminaire Nr. III, Iv, VIII, XVII, Edition Seuil (1981-1994)

Lacan, J., Die Bildungen des Unbewussten, Turia & Kant (2006)

Lacan, J., Mitschriften der Seminare,VI,IX,X,XII,XV, B.R.L.F., Strasbourg

Laplanche, J., Pontalis, J. B., Das Vokabular Der Psychoanalyse, Suhrkamp (1989)

Linke, D., Kunst und Gehirn, Rowohlt (2001)

Maar, C., Pöppel, E., Christaller, T., Die Technik auf dem Weg zur Seele, Rowohlt (1996)

Merleau-Ponty, M., Das Sichtbare und das Unsichtbare (The Visible and the Invisible) Fink Verlag (1994)

Pinker, S., Der Sprachinstinkt, Kindler (1996)

Plato, Sämtliche Werke, Insel Verlag (1991)

Popper, K. R., Eccles, J. C., Das Ich und sein Gehirn, Piper (1989)

Potthoff, P., Die Begegnung der Subjekte (The Encounter of Subjects), Psychosozial-Verlag (2014)

Roazen, D., Der innere Sinn, Archäologie eines Gefühls (The Inner Touch, Archaeology of Feeling), Fischer (2012)

Roheim, G., Die Panik der Götter (The Panic of the Gods), Kindler (1975)

Rosset, C., Das Reale in seiner Einzigartigkeit (The real in its uniqueness), Merve (2000)

Rüdinger, D., Perrez, M., Anthropologische Aspekte der Psychologie, O. Müller (1979)

Rudgley, R., Abenteuer Steinzeit, Kremaye & Scheriau (2001)

Schmidt-Hellerau, C., Lebenstrieb & Todestrieb (Life Drive & Death Drive), Libido & Lethe, Verlag Intern. Psychoanalyse (1995)

Searle, J. R., Geist, Hirn und Wissenschaft, Suhrkamp (1992)

Seidler, G. H., Der Blick des Anderen (The View of the Other), Verlag Intern, Psychoanalyse (1995)

Sinz, R., Gehirn und Gedächtnis, Fischer Utb (1981)

Strowik, E., Sprechende Körper (Speaking Bodies), Fink-Verlag (2009)

Thompson, R. F., Das Gehirn, Spectrum (1994)

Thorne, K. S., Gekrümmter Raum und Verbogene Zeit, Knaur (1996)

Tipler, F. J., Über die Omegapunkttheorie, Piper (1994)

Uexküll, Th., Fuchs, M., Subjektive Anatomie, Schattauer (1994)

Weiss, Der Andere in der Übertragung (The Other in Transference), Frommann-Holzboog, (1988)

Weizsäcker, C. F. von, Die Einheit der Natur (The Unity of Nature), Dtv (1995)

Weinberg, S., Der Traum von der Einheit des Universums, Bertelsmann (1993)

Weizenbaum, J., Die Macht der Computer, Stw (1977)

Wiener, O., Probleme der Künstlichen Intelligenz, Merve (1990)

Wilhelm, R., Informatik, C.H.Beck (1996)

Wilson, E. O., Der Wert der Vielfalt, Piper (199

Wolf, F. A., Die Physik der Träume, Byblos (1996)

Wygotski, L.S., Denken und 'Sprechen (Thinking and 'Speaking)', Fischer (1981)

Further books by the author from MCS-Verlag

Analytic Psychocatharsis

Psychoanalytic theory and cathartic meditation cannot simply be transferred into each other. If, however, both methods are related by a decisive element (formula words containing several meanings in one stroke), a new method of one's own can be established. Psychoanalysis and meditative methods are discussed, and the practice of one's own procedure is described in detail.

The Revolt of the Self

The classical method of analysis of the unconscious represents a too theoretical revolt of the self. In order to be successful in practice, a more direct self-analytic procedure is required, which everyone can develop out of themselves. Formulations that contain several meanings in a single stroke of writing can break up the unconscious of each individual through mental practice and free him or herself.

'teadrunken' The starting point of the book is the doctrine of the psychoanalyst O. Earl Wittgenstein, who assumed that man contains three parts within himself, which he can only combine in different ways to form a unity or uniform personality. He calls the ultimate and ideal unity the 'trialogue'. On the basis of the description of several mountain climbs, the author roams through all possible cultural and psychological questions in order to achieve the 'trialogue' through hiking, meditation and

Yoga and Psychoanalysis

Based on a scientific biography of the religious scientist and yoga teacher Kirpal Singh (Surat Shand Yoga), all forms of yoga are compared from the perspective of psychoanalysis. It is necessary to establish a procedure of one's own, which the author also calls *Analytic Psychocatharsis*. Numerous pictures and diagrams make the book attractive.